IMPROMPTU

IMPROMPTU

Leading in
the Moment

Judith Humphrey

WILEY

Published by John Wiley & Sons, Inc., Hoboken, New Jersey.
Published simultaneously in Canada.

For general information about our other products and services, please contact our Customer Care Department within the United States at (800) 762–2974, outside the United States at (317) 572–3993 or fax (317) 572–4002.

Wiley publishes in a variety of print and electronic formats and by print-on-demand. Some material included with standard print versions of this book may not be included in e-books or in print-on-demand. If this book refers to media such as a CD or DVD that is not included in the version you purchased, you may download this material at http://booksupport.wiley .com. For more information about Wiley products, visit www.wiley.com.

The Leader's Script® is a registered trademark of The Humphrey Group Inc.

Library of Congress Cataloging-in-Publication Data:

Names: Humphrey, Judith, 1943– author.
Title: Impromptu : leading in the moment / by Judith Humphrey.
Description: Hoboken, New Jersey : John Wiley & Sons, Inc., [2018] | Includes
    bibliographical references and index. |
Identifiers: LCCN 2017029464 (print) | LCCN 2017040994 (ebook) | ISBN
    9781119286769 (pdf) | ISBN 9781119286776 (epub) | ISBN 9781119286752
    (cloth)
Subjects: LCSH: Communication in management. | Business communication. |
    Extemporaneous speaking. | Leadership.
Classification: LCC HD30.3 (ebook) | LCC HD30.3 .H8569 2018 (print) | DDC
    658.4/092—dc23
LC record available at https://lccn.loc.gov/2017029464

Custom cover typography by Fang Yu and Ben Egnal
Cover Design: Wiley

Printed in the United States of America

10 9 8 7 6 5 4 3 2 1

To Marc
For all the impromptu moments that have
made our life together so joyous

CONTENTS

PROLOGUE

The Soul of This Book

E very book—whether autobiographical, fiction, business, or general interest—comes out of the author's inner being. Some go deeper into that place than others do. Even more than my two previous books, *Speaking as a Leader* and *Taking the Stage*, this work comes out of a very personal journey.

It all began when I was asked to give an impromptu speech in seventh grade. Our teacher thought it would be a good idea for the 12-year-olds in her class to be able to speak extemporaneously, and I was the first to be called upon. I headed to the front of the class with no small amount of trepidation, and things got worse when the topic she gave me was "boys." I vividly remember panicking because as a shy young preteen girl I certainly had thoughts about boys, but none I wanted to share publicly. Besides, talking about the opposite sex was taboo for me since I was raised in a household where we weren't even allowed to watch Elvis Presley on TV. In front of the class I somehow was able to blurt out my first line: "I don't know why you've asked me to talk about boys since I come from a family of five girls." But everything after that is a blur—I don't remember a word of it. I only remember the fear I felt in the spotlight.

I believe that episode shaped the trajectory of my career and life. Shortly after that awkward experience, I took up the violin and played on stage as often as I could to overcome my nerves. I went to a top music school, Indiana University, and continued to perform with chamber groups and orchestras. When I went on to graduate school in Rochester,

New York, I switched to literature, and then became a university lecturer in Toronto, regularly speaking before groups of several hundred
students. Eventually (after several years as a speech writer) I launched
The Humphrey Group to help other leaders overcome these fears and be
successful communicators.

It was not always easy for me to stand on these stages and play my
violin, or in later years to speak with authority and conviction. As an
undergraduate I forced myself to speak up at least once in every class. As
a university lecturer, I'd often arrive just in the nick of time—prepping
up to the last minute. As an entrepreneur, I faced down my fears when
I made cold calls to CEOs, spoke to companies about our services, or
pitched training at senior levels.

My salvation was that I practiced hard for these roles. And I've
found that the same discipline is required for all the impromptu
moments in our life. This book and its central argument—that you
need to prepare to be spontaneous—comes from all the years I've
spent working to be successful on stage and dedicating myself to
preparation, whether for a violin performance, a university lecture,
a pitch to prospective clients as an entrepreneur, a tribute speech to
family and friends, even a marriage proposal. As a result, I've come
to feel more relaxed and confident on stage—whatever that stage
may be.

Most of the speaking all of us do fits into the category of impromptu
communication. It includes all the remarks that have helped us succeed,
get our ideas across, negotiate pay raises, and build relationships with
friends and colleagues. I know how important these exchanges have
been for me. I'm certain this book will support readers in the same way.
It will give you the confidence and skills to be a superb impromptu
speaker and in so doing move toward your professional and life goals.
These key moments are not governed by a "quick fix" or "winging it."

The larger vision of this book is that discipline and preparation are the secret to successful spontaneity—and a successful life.

Judith Humphrey
Toronto, Canada

Making speeches on the spot is necessary both for those who address the people and for those who go to court and for those who take part in private gatherings ... [and] we see those who can speak [extemporaneously] honoured by others as if they had a god-like intellect.

—Alcidamas, 4th century BC

IMPROMPTU

INTRODUCTION

At the 2017 Oscars®, movie producer Jordan Horowitz provided viewers with a remarkable impromptu moment. He had just accepted the Best Picture award for *La La Land*. Suddenly there was commotion on stage, and the PricewaterhouseCoopers folks informed him that *Moonlight* had actually won. Others might have been speechless—or angry. But instead, Horowitz boldly announced: "There's a mistake. 'Moonlight,' you guys won Best Picture. This is not a joke." Then, holding up his Oscar statuette, he said: "I'm going to be really proud to hand this to my friends from 'Moonlight.'"[1]

These brief remarks were brilliant, and were justly praised by the media. Horowitz showed grace in announcing the real winner and offering up the prize so generously. Later he explained, "It was not about me. It was about making sure that 'Moonlight' got the recognition it really deserves."[2]

I'd like to think that everyone who reads this book will respond to off-the-cuff situations as eloquently as Jordan Horowitz did.

"But," you may ask, "isn't impromptu speaking something people do without thinking much about it?" The word "impromptu" conjures up the instantaneous remark, the wedding toast done in a flash of friendship, the job interview where you decided to "wing it," the insightful comment that just came into your head at a meeting. Yes, these are all acts of spontaneity. But as we know, they don't always go well. Who could be more aware of this than Tony Hayward, the BP executive who told a reporter after the explosion on the Deepwater

Horizon oil rig that "I'd like my life back." The world knew, as he did, that eleven individuals had lost their lives in the fire. His words left a bad taste—so bad that he was vilified in the media and removed from his high-profile role.[3]

And it's not just high-profile leaders who wing it and regret it. How many managers become tongue-tied when they speak up at a meeting, or go on too long, losing the thread of what they had wanted to say? How many leaders, when asked a question, ramble and conclude with a desperate, "What I'm really saying is . . .?" How many of us on conference calls wish we had been more astute and wonder if the others on the call tuned out? Who has not passed a colleague in the corridor and only afterward thought of something more meaningful to say than "How's it going?" What manager has not been stuck in the elevator with a senior executive and looked down at the floor, afraid to speak, not knowing what to say, regretting afterward the missed opportunity? And who has not spoken up at a meeting only to feel that she "lost it" in the middle of her thought?

Here's the rub: so many of us think of impromptu speaking as "winging it." That's why our corridor and watercooler conversations can sound so banal, our comments in meetings can be poorly thought out, and we can be awkward in our attempt to distill a thirty-minute PowerPoint deck into a few pithy messages when our boss says, "Just give me the big picture." It's not surprising that we have phone conversations that don't seem to go anywhere. It is not surprising that when we answer a question, we can flounder. It is, in short, not surprising that our daily conversations are often not geared to leadership and our encounters can be less than inspiring.

Impromptu speaking is an art that few have mastered. Yet it's a critical skill for leaders—not just those with fancy titles—but those at all levels who wish to come across as polished and persuasive. Impromptu speaking enables us to influence and inspire in day-to-day situations that are becoming more and more common.

What You Will Learn from This Book

The purpose of this book is to enable every reader to become much better at extemporaneous speaking. The secret is preparation! As paradoxical as it may sound, you must prepare to be spontaneous. The two statements on the cover of this book are key. "Leading in the moment" is the goal for anyone who wishes to have day-to-day impact on others. And "prepare to be spontaneous" is the means to achieving that goal.

We all have so much to say—all of us are experts in one or more fields, and we can talk endlessly if we are excited about our topic. But to say something meaningful, something motivational, something that conveys leadership on the spot, takes discipline. In some cases, you'll have only moments to collect your thoughts. In other cases, your preparation can begin well in advance of the event.

Here's a range of impromptu situations that demand some degree of preparation and forethought.

- Deciding you want to contribute to a meeting and collecting your thoughts in a few seconds.

- Sitting at a dinner event and suddenly hearing you are receiving an award (which you knew), but also hearing that you will be giving an acceptance speech (which you didn't know). You jot down a few notes on the back of a napkin.

- Attending a networking event, where you know you'll see prospective employers. You wisely polish your "elevator pitch" in advance.

- Being told you have only five minutes to give what you had thought was a thirty-minute presentation. You quickly redraft the talk to give only "the big picture."

- Seizing a moment to coach an employee and collecting your thoughts so you can leave her with a few key messages.

- Preparing for a Q&A by thinking of possible questions and developing answers.

- Finding yourself in the elevator with your boss's boss. Knowing exactly what to say because you've been thinking about how much you liked his last speech.

- Paying tribute to a departing employee with a few notes you've created.

- Being interviewed for a job and making a strong case for yourself because you've prepared notes that sell you into the role.

You won't read a script in any of these situations. You'll invent the words on the spot. But you must prepare. In fact, there needs to be just as much discipline in creating your impromptu remarks as there is in preparing for more formal speaking situations.

To lead in impromptu situations requires the right mind-set, knowledge of your material, key messages, a sound structure, clear language, and an engaging presence. All this takes preparation. In fact the word, "impromptu" derives from the Latin *in promptu* meaning "in readiness."[4] This book will show you how to be ready for all the extemporaneous situations you face every day.

Mastering the art of impromptu speaking is more important than ever in today's fast-paced, time-challenged world. Whereas decades ago you might have had weeks or months to prepare your remarks for an off-site strategy session, today such planned events are often replaced by conference calls, sometimes scheduled in a matter of minutes. And while in the past scripted speaking was the order of the day for executives and political leaders, today these staged communications are often replaced by Q&A sessions or press conferences. With the advent of social media, impromptu remarks are instantly broadcast to far-flung audiences.

Times have dramatically changed, and the stakes for these off-the-cuff comments have become very high. Those spontaneous

remarks can inspire and unite audiences, or they can wreak havoc. They can upset employees or anger voters. More than ever, there is a need to bring leadership to the impromptu stage.

This book will equip you to speak "in the moment" in ways that will convey leadership. And it will enable you to speak off the cuff in ways that will look and sound spontaneous—but will be thoughtful, well-argued, and deeply motivational.

History's Great Impromptu Speakers Were Made, Not Born

History provides many examples of individuals who faced the challenge of impromptu speaking—and discovered how to measure up to that challenge.

The first story recorded in Old English, back in the seventh century, told of a humble cowherd named Caedmon who was called upon to speak spontaneously at a mead hall feast. It was customary to pass around a harp and ask each guest to tell a story. The cowherd saw the harp coming toward him and panicked. He fled the hall in embarrassment. But he had a mystical dream that night, and when he returned to the hall he was able to miraculously compose a song of creation. All agreed it was divinely inspired.[5]

Abraham Lincoln knew the importance of spur-of-the-moment comments. He told young lawyers that: "Extemporaneous speaking should be practiced and cultivated. It is the lawyer's avenue to the public."[6] Lincoln practiced what he preached, and as a result became an extraordinary impromptu speaker as was evident in the Lincoln-Douglas debates.[7]

Winston Churchill, who would become one of the greatest orators of all time, honed his impromptu speaking skills. Early in his career he stood up to speak before the British Parliament and his mind went blank. According to a contemporary, Churchill stood there in silence "until at last he could bear it no longer; back in his seat, he could only bury his head in his hands. After his breakdown in the House

of Commons he dreaded getting up to speak more than ever."[8] But Churchill worked hard on his speaking and became an eloquent orator.

Martin Luther King, Jr., was another leader who became a remarkable extemporaneous speaker through lifelong practice. As a preacher he would think through each sermon in advance, but he didn't read from a prepared text or notes. This gave him the opportunity to "rearrange ideas on the fly even being able to pull in sections of a totally different sermon."[9] This ability to create his material in the moment was a powerful force behind his "I Have a Dream" speech. Even though he had prepared a speech the night before, the "I Have a Dream" refrain, which is the heart and soul of that address, was improvised while he was speaking. He moved the crowd in a performance that reflected his extraordinary impromptu powers.[10]

Some of today's most highly regarded business leaders have wrestled with—and overcome—stage fright, and are now superb impromptu speakers. Virgin Group's Richard Branson has spoken openly about his early traumas with speaking[11] and how he used informal phone pitches to develop his impromptu skills.[12] Tesla CEO Elon Musk has admitted that he "used to be horrendous at public speaking,"[13] and his comfort level is now with unscripted speaking. Warren Buffett said he was "terrified of public speaking,"[14] but today he speaks confidently in impromptu situations, most notably at his shareholder meetings where he is live-streamed to the entire world and fields questions for hours.[15]

Today's leaders have abundant opportunities to speak extemporaneously, and it's important to develop these skills whether you're building a business, leading an organization, expressing your political agenda, or inspiring colleagues around you.

The Power of This Book

This book focuses on the new world of communications and the opportunity to influence and inspire every day, every hour, every moment. It's for leaders. And by "leaders" I don't mean just those who

hold top positions in their organizations. I mean anyone who wishes to influence others at any level, in any capacity, inside or outside the workplace.

Impromptu: Leading in the Moment presents a single, consistent approach that works in all situations, whether you are making a point at a meeting, answering a question in the corridor, chatting at a networking event, or saying a few words at a luncheon. All these situations are platforms for your leadership. And your ability to direct the conversation toward a solution or the acceptance of an idea will serve you well as a leader. I'd also like to think that this book will inspire those who give formal speeches and PowerPoint presentations to consider impromptu speaking as a smart alternative.

The book is divided into five parts providing leaders with a roadmap for speaking impromptu.

Part I: *The New World of Impromptu* explores why extemporaneous speaking has come to dominate business life. It discusses the larger changes in organizations and how top-down structures have given way to flatter organizations in which everyone is potentially a leader and (at other times) a follower. This democratization of leadership and the movement from "big stages" to "small stages" creates enormous opportunity for those who excel at impromptu speaking.

Part II: *The Impromptu Mind-Set* explores the mental preparation required to be an effective spontaneous leader. The impromptu mind-set involves having the intention to lead, being a good listener, being authentic, being focused, and being respectful. These values and attitudes are absolutely necessary if you want to move a room—or reach one individual.

Part III: *The Leader's Script* shows you how to organize your thinking. You first need a storehouse of information and key messages to draw upon. Next comes the task of reading your audience. Once you've done that you're ready to create your script. This section sets forth the Leader's Script template for creating impromptu remarks. Its key elements are the grabber, message, structure, and call to action.

Part IV: *Impromptu Scripts for Every Occasion* offers readers templates they can use to script themselves as leaders in a full range of off-the-cuff situations. You will find scripts for meetings, job interviews, networking events, elevator conversations, micro-presentations, tributes, toasts, impromptu speeches, and Q&As.

Part V: *The Impromptu Stage* shows you how to rehearse and deliver your impromptu remarks. This involves choosing your words carefully, being "in the moment," and building rapport with your audience through the skills that improvisational actors use. In this section you will also learn how to be vocally strong and physically present in a way that engages your audience.

This book will enable you to speak as a confident leader in all off-the-cuff situations, so that you'll lead and inspire others every time you speak.

The impromptu words of tennis great, Roger Federer, offer one excellent example of how eloquent and inspirational your off-the-cuff speaking can be. After winning his eighth Wimbledon tournament in 2017, he said, "It's magical. I can't believe it yet. I guess it's just belief that I can achieve such heights." Then he explained, "I wasn't sure I was ever going to be here again in another finals after last year and I had some tough ones with Novak [Djokovic] in 2014 and 2015. But I always believed that I could maybe come back and do it again. If you believe, you can go really far in your life. I think I did that, and I'm happy that I kept on believing and dreaming and here I am today."[16]

Impromptu: Leading in the Moment will enable you to find the self-expression that takes you to these inspirational heights. You don't have to be a tennis star or a CEO to be so inspiring. You may be a manager, a team leader, or an intern. Whatever your role, every day in every conversation you will be able to motivate, lead, and inspire by taking the journey mapped out in this book.

Part I
The New World
of Impromptu

1 The Rise of Impromptu Speaking

T he way leaders communicate in organizations has undergone a remarkable transformation in the last half century. No longer is leadership delivered primarily by C-Suite executives standing behind podiums reading words written for them. Today, individuals at every level are leading with impromptu remarks. How and why that transformation has occurred provides the foundation for this book.

The Glory Days of the Formal Speech

Back in the 1980s when I entered the business world, CEOs and top executives in every organization regularly delivered formal speeches and rarely spoke spontaneously—nor was anyone else encouraged to communicate. The law of the land was for managers and junior executives to keep their mouths shut. In fact, when a group of engineers heard that we in the corporate communications department were about to introduce a program that would teach managers how to communicate, one senior engineer wrote an email, "How can we shut this program down?"

My first job as a speech writer was supporting a group of senior executives. It felt like I was joining a secret society. My boss looked me in the eye on that first day of work and said: "I'm going to turn you into a speech writer." I was a novitiate—and he was the old master passing on the secrets of this sacred craft. He sent me to New York where I took a course with one of the greats: a man who had crafted remarks for Nelson Rockefeller. When preparing a major address, there were elaborate rituals, spread over many weeks or even months. I learned to plan, research, outline, discuss, write, rewrite, and format the script for a thirty-minute talk. The CEO was involved in most of these activities, and took them very seriously. So elaborate was this process that my boss once told me that we should not agree to write a major speech if the executive did not give us at least three months to make this happen. Three months!

In those days the speech writer worked closely with the senior executive. When a CEO retired, he might pass his writer on to a friend or colleague in the industry. In fact, one retiring CEO I had been writing for called another senior executive in the industry and "offered" me as a speech writer. I didn't take the job but I was honored to have received his endorsement.

I found this work exciting, and through my affiliation with IABC (International Association for Business Communicators), I regularly presented a speech-writing course in major U.S. and Canadian cities. During these years, which were the heyday of formal speech giving, this one-day program, "The Art of Speech Writing," was often oversubscribed.

When, in 1988, I established my own communications company, The Humphrey Group, the demand for speeches was still high. Writing those speeches and coaching executives to deliver them was the bread and butter for my new firm. The demand was so great that I and my husband (an academic who regularly helped out) often worked until the wee hours of the morning to meet deadlines.

And then in the 1990s something odd but unmistakable occurred. The demand for formal speeches declined, while the number of people asking The Humphrey Group for assistance with impromptu remarks soared. I remember a conversation with a chief financial officer at that time. He had just come from speaking to analysts about the company's quarterly results. I said to him, "Where is your speech?" He pointed to his temple. I thought he was a genius to speak simply and confidently from a mental outline, but that is exactly what leaders had begun to do. The focus of leadership communications was evolving from prepared speeches to impromptu remarks.

I remember in the early 1990s coaching a senior executive—the head of engineering for a large utility—who transformed his style dramatically when he scrapped his speech and spoke from notes. In his elaborate scripted text he had highlighted certain words in yellow, in a desperate effort to draw them out. There was so much detail—numbers, information, technical data, jargon—all on the subject of metallurgical engineering. As he spoke I realized the text was dragging him down. His tone did not change from thought to thought. His pace did not change. His face was without expression. He was buried alive in all that verbiage.

I turned the videotape off and we both agreed his scripted remarks had been awful. Together we revised the text. We ditched the long, cumbersome sentences and created "memory joggers" that would remind him of his message and key points.

The transformation was remarkable. Now he was looking up, not dropping down into the text. He was talking, not reading. He embellished each point with an illustration. He was free. Free to improvise. This, I thought, was what the informal speech should be.

For good reason formal speechmaking has lost its devotees. As Bart Egnal, my successor and CEO of The Humphrey Group, says: "Over the past fifteen years that I've been with the company one trend that has never changed is the decline of formal speaking and the rise in

extemporaneous communication. The speech has died—and is being replaced by the conversation. Audiences are craving authentic conversations; formal, overly scripted performances are rejected. Leaders who take note of this trend and build their skills to capitalize on such everyday moments are winning hearts and minds."

Today more and more leaders—pressed for time and anxious to be authentic—are scrapping the script. Elon Musk, CEO of SpaceX, hired Dex Torricke-Barton, Mark Zuckerberg's speech writer, but was quick to point out in a tweet that "Dex will do comms, but my speeches are just a conversation w the audience. No time to rehearse & don't want to read from a prompter." One fan tweeted back, "That's JUST the way we like you, Elon! Off the cuff & personal." Another replied, "I agree 100%. Don't change the way you talk."[1]

This transformation of leadership communications from scripts to spontaneity, from the big stage to the small stage, reflects a new era of impromptu speaking.

The Three Reasons for the Rise of Impromptu Speaking

The rise in impromptu speaking (and the decline of formal addresses) reflects three closely related developments that have changed our world.

First, the Flattening of Organizations

Businesses large and small, governments at all levels, charities, and even volunteer associations are very different than they were twenty (or even ten) years ago. There's still someone at the "top." But there are now fewer layers, and fewer barriers between top and bottom. Knowledge and decision-making are decentralized.

The change that emerged in the 1990s was a long time in coming. Deborah Ancona, a professor of management and organizational

studies at MIT, chronicles an evolution that began with the "super bureaucracies" of the 1920s. And while there were modifications in the intervening decades, the most significant changes have occurred in recent years. The result has been today's workplace with "what's called variously eco-leadership, collaborative leadership, or distributed leadership."[2]

As Ancona and Henrik Bresman explain in their book, *X-Teams*, "The shift from a singular reliance on command-and-control leadership to more of a distributed leadership mind-set requires additional dialogue and alignment up and down the organization."[3] That's because "critical knowledge and information that used to flow vertically from the top is now flowing not only both ways but also laterally across units and organizations."[4] Everyone now is expected to bring forward their ideas and inspire followers. Communications are no longer the sole responsibility of those at the top. Leadership is expected at all levels of the organization. Even a junior analyst must be able to present a clear summary of his thinking to someone who might be a C-Suite executive or a portfolio manager. Nobody gets off the hook! Leadership does not reside in a title. It exists in this ability to inspire people up, down, and across the organization.

Today's leaders must communicate in a more open, authentic, and informal manner than was previously done at the top. This approach requires listening, consensus-building, and collaboration in meetings, one-on-one encounters, and parking lot or elevator conversations. Leadership is based on everyday encounters where one feels the need to lead in the moment, speak spontaneously, and share an idea or a vision of what's possible. This is leadership in the organizations of the twenty-first century.

Second, the Power of Technology

Technology has accelerated the shift to distributed leadership. For the longest time knowledge was the exclusive domain of the few individuals

at the top. In the nineteenth and the first part of the twentieth century the CEO and his circle (invariably men) received the reports from an army of accountants and bookkeepers. That exclusivity did not end with the advent of mainframes in the 1950s. Still relatively few individuals had access to information.

But all that changed beginning in the 1990s with the rise of the World Wide Web and low-cost networked computers. Almost overnight every knowledge worker had access to extraordinary amounts of information. In *The Cluetrain Manifesto,* the authors argue that the Internet has transformed organizations from a structure based on hierarchies to one based on distributed knowledge: "Org charts worked in an older economy where plans could be fully understood from atop steep management pyramids and detailed work orders could be handed down from on high. Today, the org chart is hyperlinked, not hierarchical. Respect for hands-on knowledge wins over respect for abstract authority."[5]

With technology everyone has access to everyone else. Emailing, messaging, texting, blogging, tweeting, and conference calls provide nonhierarchical channels of communication. Even CEOs now use Facebook as a way of reaching their employees. As Paul Vallée, CEO of Pythian, a global IT services company, told me: "I post on Facebook four or five times a day. And almost everything I post is about unlocking the potential in others. Pythian has people in 155 cities around the world. Facebook lets me reach them and other groups I support."

Technology has created a whole new environment for communication. "Technology starts the human conversation much faster and transforms it into a global conversation," according to Murray Wigmore, vice president of sales for Panasonic Healthcare Corp. of North America. He told me: "I live and breathe the health care market. Let's say someone in our industry says, 'Hey, we have a customer who's developing a new product.' This news would spread around the world through the web. The next communication is from someone

who picks up the phone from somewhere in the world and wants to talk. That leads to a teleconference or videoconference, and the voice on the call replaces the fancy PowerPoint slides that used to define the conversation. The human voice has replaced pictures, and given rise to spontaneous communications." Technology has reinvented the way we communicate in organizations.

Hence the link between technology and impromptu. People are communicating in shorter, more spontaneous, and more authentic ways, making impromptu speaking more the norm than the exception. As well, thanks to technology everybody in an organization is a little more familiar with everyone else. So let's say a manager sees the CEO in an elevator, she's more likely to say, "How did your speech go?" Or if a sales executive has brought in a new client, he is more apt to share this good news with others in the elevator.

Technology and its empowerment of employees have also created team-based organizations. At Google, executive Diane Greene notes, top executives are "emailing and talking and meeting and coordinating constantly now." This development means that "We all have a really clear understanding of what we're doing, why we're doing it, and what we're trying to achieve."[6] And this collaboration takes place at all levels. As David Hahn, managing director of New York media relations firm Media Connect, observes, "Everybody is working in teams so there's a lot more familiarity with people across departments and in your own department. A CEO might be on a pitch team or a strategy meeting. That whole flattening means more familiarity, more informality, and more impromptu moments."

Thomas Petzinger, Jr., of the *Wall Street Journal*, writes in the Foreword to *The Cluetrain Manifesto*: "This book shows how conversation forms the basis of business, how business lost that voice for a while, and how that language is returning to business thanks to a technology that inspires, and in many cases demands, that we speak from the heart."[7]

Third, a New Sense of Time and Space

The third factor in the emergence of impromptu speaking is the recalibration of time and space. Thanks to our interconnected world, time zones have dissolved and we live in a 24/7 universe. Virtually every company is affected by fluctuations in financial markets or news stories that happen halfway around the globe.

The flow of information, once a trickle, has become a veritable Niagara Falls of emails, texts, news reports, videos, and social media posts. Research indicates that workers dedicate 28 hours a week to emails—writing, reading, or responding to them. And the average person checks his or her smartphone 150 times a day.[8] This leaves less time for lengthy, formal events, with the result that older forms of communication (speeches, presentations, meetings) have been replaced by crisp impromptu exchanges. In fact, impromptu speaking has become the modus operandi for leaders, reflecting the fact that everything leaders do is chopped up, fragmented into short bits of activity.

David Hahn regularly "huddles" with Media Connect team members in chats that last three to five minutes. He finds these more efficient than regular meetings, and the spontaneous huddles give him and his team members an opportunity to have a quick dialogue and move a project forward. Rory Cowan, CEO of Lionbridge Technologies, a Waltham, Massachusetts, technology services firm with about 4,500 employees, says that instead of spending a lot of time in long face-to-face meetings, he spends more time "doing frequent iterative touches," either in person or via text message, instant messaging, and video chat—sometimes with "four or five windows open concurrently."[9] If an employee wants to talk to her boss, she's more likely to poke her head into her boss's office for a quick impromptu exchange than wait to get on his calendar.

A University of California study revealed that work fragmentation is common, both because people spend less time on individual tasks

and because they are interrupted more frequently. On average, those interviewed spent just eleven minutes, four seconds on a task before switching to another activity or being interrupted.[10] No wonder business leaders find impromptu conversations better suited to today's environment.

Even the physical structure of our offices furthers this bombardment of information and fragmentation of activity. Michael Bloomberg, CEO of Bloomberg Inc., believes in transparency and his desk is in an open space on the fifth floor of the Bloomberg building.[11] Mark Zuckerberg has an office that is glassed in and on the same sprawling floor where project teams reside in a "building as village" concept.[12] The typical office is now designed around a more open concept, encouraging—for better or for worse—interruptions by colleagues who ask, "Do you have a minute?" or "Can you answer a quick question?" The new spaces also include chat rooms, as well as snack bars, kitchens, recreational facilities, and other areas that encourage conversation. As architect Jennifer Magnolfi writes: "The best practices [in office design today] are emerging from the world of coworking spaces, hacker spaces, maker spaces—environments that are designed around core principles of openness, sharing, and co-creation."[13] As a result of all these emerging realities in the workplace, communications have become more spontaneous. A more informal, impromptu style has become the norm. We in The Humphrey Group have seen this in our work with clients. A CFO replaced his one-hour PowerPoint presentation to analysts with a five-minute overview, followed by fifty-five minutes of questions and answers. It's no longer a speech. It's a conversation.

A senior vice president we work with had just joined a new firm and was asked to speak at the next town hall to three thousand employees. He did what most responsible executives would do: He carefully prepared a scripted speech. When his CEO saw him lay his script on the podium during a rehearsal, he asked, "What's that?"

"It's my speech," the new executive replied.

"Oh, we don't give speeches here," the CEO said. "Just talk to our employees."

Fortunately he had time to mentally master the thoughts he had written out, and he spoke without a text to rave reviews.

Those who want to succeed must learn to lead in the moment—this goes for leaders at every level. No more speeches from on high. Just simple, heartfelt conversations with audiences—and if these remarks are not entirely spontaneous, they need to look and sound spontaneous.

Not only are leaders speaking more informally, but they are speaking more frequently to individuals at all levels in the organization—up, down, and across. They talk with customers and contacts outside their companies too. Here are typical requests we get from people who want to be better leaders.

- An analyst wants to know how to talk to his CEO at the coffee machine.
- A vice president wishes to be better at "small talk" so she can network with clients.
- A manager wants to share his ideas with his CEO without sounding presumptuous.
- An HR staff member wants to speak confidently to her boss's boss in the elevator.
- A tech CEO wants to listen to his team and their ideas—rather than jumping in.
- A team leader needs help with "difficult conversations." She has an employee who keeps arriving late and missing meetings.
- A bright financial wiz wants to share his ideas at meetings, but his tendency to talk too much is turning off his colleagues.

Speaking in meetings, corridors, elevators, offices, on the phone, and in a host of other settings is an exacting process. To be successful, a leader must read her audience, anticipate any questions or concerns, create a script on the spot that drives home a point, and deliver it with sincerity and political savvy. Even when there's time to prepare, the speaker must sound "spontaneous" and not scripted.

More than ever those who lead must find their authentic voice. It's no longer acceptable—or effective—to rely on jargon that once defined "corporate speak." Today's leaders need to get real, be authentic, and do so in all situations. They need a warm, conversational style that works in the new organization where everyone is connected and everyone is expected to be open and sincere.

Impromptu speaking provides a way to connect, inspire, and lead in the twenty-first-century world. Scripted speeches, PowerPoint presentations, dog and pony shows, and marketing hype are being replaced by the conversations that leaders have every day with their followers. These conversations will change minds, hearts, and organizations.

2 Power of Spontaneity

Larry Page, cofounder of Google, walked up to a stranger at a conference and began a dialogue with him. The stranger was Charles Chase, an engineer who manages Lockheed Martin's nuclear fusion program. According to the *New York Times*, "They spent 20 minutes discussing how much time, money and technology separated humanity from a sustainable fusion reaction—that is, how to produce clean energy by mimicking the sun's power—before Mr. Chase thought to ask the man his name."

> "I'm Larry Page," he said. Chase was stunned to know he'd been talking to the head of Google.
>
> "He didn't have any sort of pretension like he shouldn't be talking to me or 'Don't you know who you're talking to?' Mr. Chase said. 'We just talked.'"[1]

Such spontaneous, nonhierarchical dialogue is the new narrative for business leaders. No longer hidden behind podiums, today's leaders are more likely to engage in interviews, town halls, elevator conversations, or brief exchanges sparked by "Do you have a minute?" These dialogues provide leaders with rich opportunities to achieve so much more than they were able to achieve when they simply stood behind a podium to deliver an annual "address."

Below are the ways impromptu speaking has compelling power for leaders.

Abundant Opportunities

Informal conversations are everywhere—in the office, elevators, restrooms, corridors, parking lots, meeting rooms, chat rooms, cafeterias, restaurants, airplanes, golf courses, and every other place you can imagine. A business leader can run into a boss or an employee in any of these settings. When I surveyed clients, asking them, "How many impromptu leadership moments do you have in a day?" Here's what they said:

- "I have a TON. That's really what I do."
- "Ninety percent of my discussions are unscripted."
- "Every day I have twenty to twenty-three impromptu leadership moments."
- "I'll have about two each hour. That's twenty in a ten-hour day."
- "You're a leader in your work, in your family, in your community. You don't ever get to turn that responsibility off. So, my answer is, all the time."

These responses suggest that every leader has many opportunities every day to inspire and influence. In fact we have many moments *in each hour* when we are interrupted.[2] The best leaders regard these not as "interruptions," but as opportunities to reach and motivate people.

And this frequency is important. People don't necessarily "get" what you want them to if you say it only once. You need to repeat your messages over and over and over again. In impromptu settings you can do just that—in the corridor, the elevator, the lunchroom, the meeting room, and the office. Each time you repeat your message it will sound fresh and spontaneous, and over time you will have the impact you want.

Collaborating—Up, Down, and Across the Organization

Spontaneous conversations bring people at different ranks and in different areas of a firm together and allow them to share ideas. Technology and open offices have put everyone in touch with everyone else. That's why impromptu exchanges have become so important. They collapse hierarchies and bridge areas of expertise.

The old approach of delivering a platform speech or issuing executive announcements lacked interactivity. It's a top-down approach that doesn't work anymore. Knowledge and insight—whether about fusion reaction or customer solutions—is distributed among the minds of many people at many levels. The new style of communicating allows you to develop bonds up, down, and across the organization.

If a manager sees her CEO in the elevator she can ask, "What did you think of the email I sent you?" or "Can we chat about an idea I have?" Such conversations open doors and advance careers. It's also important for leaders to seize opportunities to speak openly and frequently to their teams. That's because there is more uncertainty in today's rapidly changing workplace, and people are thirsty for information. Without such knowledge, rumors and speculation spread. Impromptu speaking is a way to disseminate solid information throughout the organization, and make employees feel more comfortable in their work environment. Such conversations help an organization to remain in sync. As Boris Groysberg, co-author of *Talk, Inc.*, says: "I think the speed of change, how industries are changing, how products are changing, is much, much faster than it used to be. So staying close to customers, staying close to your employees, that's becoming more and more important."[3]

Impromptu conversations can stimulate collaborative idea sharing. "Ideas typically do not just come to you," Mark Zuckerberg said in a 2014 Q&A session at Facebook. "They happen because you've been talking about something or thinking about something and talking to

a lot of people about it for a long period of time."[4] Zuckerberg draws inspiration "from his coterie of senior managers" and "is constantly stress-testing his hypotheses" with those around him.[5]

Faster, Better Decision-Making

Spontaneous conversations allow you to resolve problems and give feedback on a more timely basis. Brief, on-the-fly meetings have become the order of the day. Ian Gordon, senior vice president of brands for Loblaw Companies, a Canadian food retailer, says that his "impromptu leadership moments enable faster decisions." He works in an office with thousands of employees, and remarks, "I walk around and have short interactions—thirty seconds to thirty minutes—with the people doing the work. These conversations often bring clarity to a situation that the employee has been wrestling with."

Sundar Pichai, Google's CEO, often meets with Google employees in a room next to his office that has been nicknamed "Sundar's Huddle." On one such occasion, according to an article in *Fast Company*, the group had "barely begun its presentation when Pichai starts peppering [participants] with questions, opinions, and advice. For half an hour the discussion careens from subject to subject."[6] This is the power of impromptu, on-the-fly exchanges that lead to better decision-making.

The best managers encourage such encounters. One executive told me: "When it comes to meetings with my boss, impromptu is the way to move things forward. Right now, to get an hour of my boss's time I need to schedule it eight weeks out. But I can meet him in the hall to cover off what I need to know in less than five minutes. I get stopped all the time in the halls, too, by my people who often hang out near my office so they can ask for a few minutes of my time." Impromptu speaking has become the most efficient way to move a business agenda forward. So the next time your staff member says, "Do you have a moment?" instead of saying, "Can it wait?" say, "Of course ... what is it?"

The traditional performance review, too, has been scaled back to create more timely feedback and development. Some forward-looking organizations are replacing annual reviews with mentoring and coaching moments in which leaders provide short bursts of feedback.

Miyo Yamashita, the managing partner of talent and workplace at Deloitte, told me in a recent conversation, "Deloitte has moved away from the annual performance review and performance ratings to regular face-to-face check-ins between employees and their managers. Rather than filling out a lengthy questionnaire once a year and writing a plan," explains Yamashita, "we now ask our people to answer five short questions in what we call a pulse survey. Managers also fill in what we call performance snapshots once a quarter or even as regularly as every several weeks." "The beauty of this new approach," says Yamashita, is that "we're creating regular mentoring and coaching moments."

GE, too, is creating a faster feedback loop. As Chairman and CEO Jeff Immelt explained: "We're trying to end anything that was annual or quarterly and make everything more real-time. . . . Instead of an annual employee review, we have an app PD@GE where our people are getting continuous insights from their colleagues that they can use to get better every day."[7]

A New Way to Get Close

Impromptu exchanges bring leaders and their listeners closer together than in the old days of podiums and pontification. The authors of *The Cluetrain Manifesto* explain this new world of communication: "Many of those drawn into this world find themselves exploring a freedom never before imagined: to indulge their curiosity, to debate, to disagree, to laugh at themselves, to compare visions, to learn, to create new art, new knowledge."[8]

Off-the-cuff interactions provide a powerful dynamic, because they are dialogues with our audience; traditional communications took

the form of monologues. Audience feedback helps a leader define clear and powerful messages. Dr. Allan Conway, former dean of the Odette School of Business, University of Windsor, says: "I'll walk into a classroom with three potential ways that I will deliver a lecture. I don't know how I'm going to do it until I actually start the class and see the students' eyes." My husband, a university professor, tells of a colleague who dazzled his undergraduate classes by building his lectures on the spot, in what amounted to a virtual dialogue with his students. He knew his subject cold, but instead of creating a script in advance, he would read the room, see what their eyes and body language told him, and develop his script in response to what he saw.

Achieving this rapport with your audience in your daily business life requires a new way of thinking—seeing encounters as moments to "open up" and engage in true dialogue rather than "chitchat." For many leaders sharing ideas still seems to be stuck in the realm of bigger forums. The concept that somehow a manager or a boss at 10:30 on an average morning can approach a direct report and share a vision doesn't seem to exist. Leaders have not quite figured out how to fit big-picture thinking into their everyday business lives. They're busy with the operational, the technical, and the tactical. They need to see that five-minute conversation as an opportunity to genuinely connect with those they work with.

So the next time you pass a staff member in the hall, share something deeper and offer them more than "Hi, how's it going?" Tell them what you're thinking—share a vision—and ask for their views. The dialogue just might surprise you with its brilliance. By promoting dialogue, informal remarks connect speakers to their audiences—and for leaders that means closer ties to employees, clients, bosses, and everyone they work with.

Being Real, Being Trustworthy

Spontaneous speaking allows you to be authentic and trustworthy—no small benefit when you are leading a team or organization. It's for this reason that Patrick Lencioni urges leaders not to "wordsmith [their] messages to death and make themselves sound like robotic leaders going out to read from the same exact script. Instead, they need to get clear on the main points to communicate and then go to their teams to explain these points in their own words."[9] When leaders speak in an unscripted mode, their tones are more genuine and their listeners know they're speaking from the heart, not from a text that someone else might have written for them.

This approach is particularly important when a company is talking about critical issues that affect employees—such as mergers or layoffs. As one SVP put it, "You get a large, rather impersonal announcement from 'head office' and people are on edge. But if you can deliver that message in an impromptu way, and understand every constituent's concern, you can really shape the message and address their concerns, so the message is more relevant to them. You can really make a difference in the way those messages are received."

I personally have felt the power of impromptu speaking in building trust. When I promoted my first book, *Speaking as a Leader*, I gave speeches, presentations, and webinars about the book. But when promoting my second book, *Taking the Stage: How Women Can Speak Up, Stand Out, and Succeed*, I chose an "on-stage conversation," which created audience trust. Typically, the one to two hundred women and a few brave men in the audience soon became part of that on-stage conversation and openly shared their concerns, goals, fears, and hopes. Some even came forward and took some coaching from me in front of the larger audience. It's as though the conversation on stage and

the conversation with the larger audience blended into one, creating a natural and relaxed atmosphere in which the audience felt they could open up.

Some of Your Best Lines

Impromptu speaking can produce some of your best lines. Although spontaneous comments can be disastrous when delivered by an individual who is unprepared or simply lacks sensitivity, when spoken by a leader who has prepped for the event and brings grace and gravitas, such remarks can be captivating.

John F. Kennedy's biographer, Theodore Sorensen, wrote that "[Kennedy's] spontaneous remarks were consistently more effective than his prepared texts." Sorensen explains that "In one talk, speaking hurriedly with a few notes and little sleep, he repeated the same phrase three times in a single sentence. The crowd laughed, and so did Kennedy. 'We are going to put this speech to music,' he told them, 'and make a fortune out of it.'"[10]

Many of the most powerful movie lines have been ad-libbed—created on the spot by actors who no doubt surprised the director, and surprised themselves with brilliant lines that came from being centered on their role. Humphrey Bogart's "Here's looking at you, kid," in *Casablanca* was first spoken off camera while he was teaching Ingrid Bergman how to play poker, then it came out spontaneously during the shooting of the movie. Robert De Niro ad-libbed the line "Are you talkin' to me?" in *Taxi Driver*. In fact he improvised that entire scene. Jack Nicholson in *A Few Good Men* ad-libbed "You can't handle the truth!" a vast improvement over the scripted line, "You already have the truth." And in *The Devil Wears Prada*, Meryl Streep got inside the head of her character, fashion editor Miranda Priestly, with the memorable ad-lib: "Oh, don't be ridiculous, Andrea, everybody wants this. Everybody wants to be us."[11]

Who has not felt that some of their best leadership moments have been impromptu? It might be a witty retort at a meeting, a comeback that earns a "touché" from your colleagues, or a moving thank-you speech when you've been surprised by your team or a family member. I had such an experience when my husband threw a surprise birthday party for me. There were about sixty guests in a Mexican-themed party, and I was moved by the fact that he had kept it a secret and so many friends had surprised me. In my impromptu remarks I thanked my husband, colleagues, and friends. The speech was one of my best. Could I have prepared it in advance if I'd known about the party? Not a chance, because—and this is one of the most important reasons impromptu speaking has such power—the situation sparks your best lines. The secret is to get inside the part you're playing and connect with the people you're talking to.

Charismatic Leadership

The crowning touch of impromptu speaking is that it will make you charismatic. According to research published in *Psychological Science*, people who respond to questions or statements without hesitation come across as charismatic. "When we looked at charismatic leaders, musicians, and other public figures, one thing that stood out is that they are quick on their feet," said the researchers.[12] And this ability to react without hesitation is attractive to others. As Julie Beck writes in *The Atlantic*, "The rapid-fire back and forth of a witty repartee is an exhilarating thing. When the conversation is ping-ponging between you and someone else—be it on a date, or in a business meeting, or at happy hour—chances are you'll find yourself drawn to that person."[13]

Impromptu speaking does require mental speed. No one will listen to you if you talk on and on, or overelaborate your point. When you are on the impromptu stage, people expect you to get to your point quickly

and show them why you believe what you're saying. But this kind of charisma comes from more than quick-mindedness. It also comes from being able to interact successfully with others. As Stephen T. Asma, jazz musician and professor at Columbia College, writes: "The key to successful improvisation is getting your *self* out of the way. Usually the ego tries to coordinate everything, but good improvisers dial down the ego and let the embodied system act, play and respond with reduced ego supervision. In the lingo of recent cognitive science, improv reduces the brain's 'executive control' function, allowing the more associational mind to take over."[14]

If you are the kind of leader who can pass someone in the hall, grab their attention, offer a quick insight, listen, respond, then move on, you will have the charisma people are looking for. And it will be something you can express every day as a leader.

There is enormous power for all of us in impromptu speaking. As the world gets faster and more complex, leaders have to use every impromptu opportunity to engage and enlighten their colleagues, their teams, their management, their customers, friends, and family. Impromptu speaking allows us to break out of traditional structures, facilitate better, faster, and more collaborative decisions, and share our ideas and feelings with those we care about … those we choose to lead.

Part II
The Impromptu
Mind-Set

3 Be Intent on Leading

Good impromptu speaking is a matter of words, scripts, and presence. But before those words can be selected or scripts formed, there is a need to bring the right mind-set. And that's what this section of the book is all about. The right mind-set includes having the intention to lead, being a good listener, and being authentic, focused, and respectful. Get your outlook right, and you'll find the other pieces will fall into place.

The most successful executives and managers see every encounter as a potential leadership moment. In this new world of spontaneous communications, an opportunity to lead might come at any moment, in any situation, at any level, to anyone in the organization. Each time you meet another employee, colleague, executive, customer, supplier, or business associate there is a potential "leadership moment"—a moment to influence, inspire, or move others to action.

But you must have the *intention* to lead. This involves the *desire* to move others by shaping their opinions, influencing their actions, or just connecting with them on a human level and making them feel better about their workplace or their lives. Seizing these opportunities means, above all, realizing the potential of your own leadership and the ever-present opportunity to have an impact on others. And in a world where the majority of employees say they are "not engaged" or "actively disengaged" in their jobs and "emotionally disconnected" from their

workplaces, there is every reason to reach out continually to people at all levels.[1]

Steve Jobs had an almost compulsive intention to lead. The quality often associated with him was his "intensity."[2] "Intention" and "intensity" are in the same family. This determination to lead cannot be turned on and off. It is part of our DNA as leaders. True leaders approach every situation with the goal of making every interaction a leadership moment. If that constancy of purpose feels obsessive to you, it won't feel that way to others, because each person experiences your leadership as a distinct act—a gift to them.

Paul Vallée, CEO of Pythian, a global IT services company, told me that when he walks down the corridor he sees many leadership opportunities: "Even if I just have a moment as I pass a customer in the hall, I can instill in that person a sense of comfort with us, and that customer may call us back in a month or two to talk. That's a leadership moment. Or if I am walking down the corridor and see an employee, and take the time to smile and address that employee by name, perhaps invite him into my office and ask what his plans are for the weekend, that's a leadership moment, because that openness and connection will make that employee feel more engaged, and my vision is to have happy, engaged, and productive employees."

When you are intent on leading you'll get results: engaged customers, employees, colleagues, and internal clients. But this does not mean you buttonhole everyone you pass in the corridor, or get in the face of every executive riding an elevator. As Bart Egnal, CEO of The Humphrey Group says, "One mistake leaders can make in impromptu conversations is to assume that because every interaction *could* be a leadership moment every interaction *should* be one. You need to pick your spots."

Smart leaders know when to seize leadership moments. Here are the ways to identify your best leadership opportunities.

Pick the Right Time and Place

When it comes to timing, don't speak too soon or wait too long to share your ideas. Marissa Mayer, CEO of Yahoo!, jumped the gun in January 2016 when she spoke about layoffs. People were already skittish about rumored layoffs, but she quipped during an all-company meeting, "There are going to be no layoffs *this week*."[3] She chose a poor time to get into a sensitive topic (and joking about it didn't help!). A month later the company did announce layoffs of 1,500 employees. Her remark hurt employee morale.

On the other hand, waiting too long to bring your people into the loop about company plans can cause the rumor mill to work overtime and create confusion among employees. Patrick Lencioni, in his book *The Advantage,* writes: "The world is full of organizations where employees feel uninformed and in the dark even though they have access to more glossy newsletters, interactive Web sites, and overly produced employee meetings than they need or want."[4] Giving your people a "heads-up" about a company decision, a new direction, or even the arrival of a new team member is critical.

Choose your setting, too. Public spaces are not the best for sensitive discussions. Suppose a manager has become annoyed that a member of his team is regularly late for work. One day he passes this employee in the hall at 9:15, as that individual is heading into work. The manager sarcastically says, "Late again, Phil?" This is the wrong place to raise this issue—it's public, it doesn't provide an opportunity for a full discussion, and the passing comment will only create further tension. A closed-door talk would be much better.

Collect Your Thoughts

Great impromptu speakers don't sputter out their thoughts with "um's" and "ah's," but they begin with immediate clarity. When Justin

Trudeau, Canada's youthful prime minister, took office on November 4, 2015, he showed this ability to collect his thoughts. When asked, "Why is it so important for you to have a gender-balanced cabinet?" he responded decisively, "Because it's 2015."[5] His comment connected him to a younger generation and underscored his commitment to women. This comment went viral and earned him a reputation as a leader with a quick, sharp mind.

Politicians and their staff typically devote considerable time to crafting and practicing responses to questions they suspect the media may ask following a major announcement. In this case, Trudeau and his advisers must have known someone was bound to ask a question about gender balance in the new cabinet, and very likely prepared this great sound bite for Trudeau to "hit it out of the park" when the question came. You don't have to have Justin Trudeau's rapid-fire eloquence, but you should at the very least collect your thoughts before speaking.

This is perhaps the most difficult challenge for impromptu speakers. After all, you may have only seconds to collect your thoughts. There is a tendency among all of us to disgorge whatever is in our mind at the time. This may be an information dump, or worse still, it may be a thought that would have been better shelved in the recesses of our mind. A criticism of another person or a half-baked observation about a topic being discussed may require damage control. The solution: think first . . . then speak.

Have Your Audience's Full Attention

You can't act as a leader if no one is listening. Even if you have something powerful to say, or feel the person you are reaching out to knows you're there, don't speak until you have the undivided attention of the people you're talking to. That doesn't require the cloistered space of a private office. But it does mean you have to have the ear of your listener or listeners, whether in a corridor, cafeteria, or conference room.

An HR professional told me she saw such an opportunity in a cafeteria line. She had just come back from a leadership training program, and found herself lining up for lunch next to the senior executive who had sponsored this training program. It had been a wonderful week of learning and growing for her. She told him: "I'm just back from our Leadership Bootcamp Program, and I can't thank you enough for sponsoring this program." A hearty conversation ensued, and that leadership moment proved important for her career.

The same holds true when you are in a meeting. Wait until you have the full attention of the room before making your point. Getting that attention can be challenging. Stay in the "ready" position and seize that moment when there's a pause in the conversation. Once you speak, claim that attention—hold on to it by speaking with conviction, with a tone of voice that says, "I've got something important to tell you." Your audience will take their cue from you.

The toughest situation for getting the attention of the "room" is conference calls. One client told me of a frustrating conference call in which she was pitching an idea from Montreal to a group of far-flung listeners—some were in Las Vegas eating breakfast in a conference room, others were in New York City trying to work on a press release, and still others were listening from India. What could she have done to make sure everyone was listening?

In addition to speaking with a strong, clear voice, she should have engaged her audience by creating an interactive dialogue. When you're in this situation, refer to participants by name, as in "Jim, I know this approach will meet your needs." Or call out groups: "Those of you in New York will appreciate the scope of this offering." And ask questions to engage your listeners: "How many of you have encountered this challenge?" These techniques work even if you're all in the same room, but they're particularly important if you are in different locations.

Have Something Valuable to Say

Every time you put your hand up or open your mouth to speak, you should have something to say that's worthy of people's attention and worthy of your role. If you don't have something of substance, keep quiet and listen to others.

Abraham Lincoln was one of the great orators of modern times. The world knows that his Gettysburg Address was a well-crafted and memorable speech, but Lincoln also spoke eloquently off the cuff. Yet he only spoke when he had something of value to say. When visitors lined the streets the night before his famous Gettysburg Address and asked Lincoln to say a few words, he responded by saying, "I appear before you, fellow-citizens, merely to thank you for this compliment. . . . I have no speech to make. In my position it is somewhat important that I should not say any foolish things."[6]

One of the most frequent complaints about unskilled impromptu speakers is that they "like the sound of their own voices," and "fill the room with hot air." I once coached an individual who had the well-earned reputation among his colleagues of being a talker—they nicknamed him "Andrew Blowhard." Everyone tried to keep him from talking in meetings by not asking him any questions. Eyes rolled as he babbled on.

Leaders do not waste others' time. They speak clearly, passionately, and to the point. Any time someone pitches a timely idea, makes a persuasive case, or moves others to action, that individual will have met the requirement of delivering something of value. And it doesn't have to be an executive preaching to the masses. It might be a manager, analyst, or an executive assistant who has a compelling idea and knows how to get it across to her audience. Success will come to those who believe in their ideas and put them forward. When you have a valuable contribution, you'll find knowledge-hungry executives eager to listen.

Build a Relationship

Seize a leadership moment to strengthen a relationship with a colleague, a boss, a mentor, a client, or someone in your network.

A young woman told me that she wanted to build a better relationship with an internal client. She changed the route she took to her desk in the morning so she could pass by the client's desk. Every day she would make a point of smiling and saying, "Good morning." At first there was little reaction. But gradually she began to get a smile back. So she added more personal touches like, "How was your weekend?" or "We should have lunch some time." The client began to nod her head, and these conversations led to a warmer and more productive relationship.

Building relationships as a leader also involves identifying people who need to feel valued. One vice president told me, "When I'm riding up in the elevator with associates or younger staff I say, 'How are things going? Are you working on anything new? Are you enjoying your job?' I try to show them that I am genuinely interested in what they are doing. These are opportunities to build a relationship with them and demonstrate leadership."

But don't overload the conversation with leadership moments. As Bart Egnal of The Humphrey Group explains: "If you've just spent a day with your team talking strategy, don't make the dinner that night a rehash. If you've just briefed your CEO on your capital program, spare her your key message while you're on a coffee break. Know when your audience will be receptive to your thinking and when they will not."

Be Face-to-Face

Person-to-person conversations are far more effective than paper communications, electronic communications, or social media. So if you want to lead, do your best to be in front of your listener.

Mary Vitug, a Managing Director in Equity Capital Markets for a major bank, put it well in a conversation with me: "In today's business world there is a lot of emphasis on faceless communications. Email, texts, phones. That makes face-to-face communications so much more important. That's when you can communicate feelings and build trust. In-person meetings let you show clients how committed you are to them. In my business you can't ignore these potential leadership moments."

It's also best to go face-to-face when you aspire to earn the confidence of an executive or manager. This was the advice given by Phil Mesman, a portfolio manager and partner at Picton Mahoney, a Canadian asset management firm. He explained to me that he was approached by a young analyst who wanted to know how to get ahead in his career. Mesman said, "You've got to get in front of the people you want to influence. It's not enough to send an email. You have to really sell yourself face-to-face to have people care about you and the portfolios you manage." Leadership moments come to those who have the courage to get in front of decision makers and sell themselves.

Be Politically Sensitive

Even though organizations are flatter today, there are still political protocols for leading up, down, and across your organization. And that means impromptu conversations must be undertaken with sensitivity. Leading from below is the most difficult, and your intent to lead must be done without sounding either fawning or presumptuous. If you are speaking with someone several steps below you in the company, warmth and candor are appreciated, condescension is not. And if you are speaking "across" the organization do not encroach on someone else's territory.

The message is this: Be careful to respect people's positions. My son, Ben, is a young art director in an advertising firm. He and his agency

were doing great work for a company where I know the head of sales. I said to my son one day, "Why don't you grab a coffee with Paul, who heads up sales. You might be able to find out more about their advertising needs."

He responded, "I better check with my boss first." A week later I asked him how the conversation had gone. He filled me in, showing his political savvy in not rushing into that meeting: "My boss said we should probably have our account managers handle that side of the relationship. They know the client and all the key players. But thanks anyway, Mom."

I'm sharing this story because anyone who works in an organization needs to have a deep understanding of the lines of authority. Lack of political savvy can be a deterrent to career success.

Realize the Mic Is Always On

Leaders must realize that any words they deliver in meetings—even behind closed doors—can be broadcast to other audiences.

When you're out with your friends or colleagues for an after-hours drink, remember the phrase "walls have ears" and don't say anything that you would not like to see repeated when it travels beyond those walls (as it will!). Even a seemingly innocent offhanded remark about a colleague like, "He's got issues," can easily make its way back to the office.

Every leader needs to keep this "mic-is-on" mentality. In 2016 a spokesperson for Carrier, a firm owned by United Technologies, told a gathering of employees that the company would be moving 1,400 jobs from the United States to Mexico.[7] There was a strong emotional reaction from employees in the room—with booing and shouting and anger. A video of the company's announcement—taken by someone in the audience—went viral, showing the emotional reaction

of employees. What began as a low-key, in-company announcement became a scandal with international and political repercussions.

Assume that anything you say will move beyond the walls where you are speaking. As Rosabeth Moss Kanter writes about leadership in the Internet age, *"E-culture is like living in a glass house under a huge spotlight that's always on, 24/7.* Mistakes are immediately visible and magnified."[8] Indeed, today as never before, impromptu comments from political leaders can worsen (or improve) domestic conflicts, drive global markets—or shape international relations. Sound bites that might appear forceful and catchy can resonate in world capitals and easily be misconstrued. All the more reason for evaluating each of these leadership opportunities, and viewing them in the context of broader agendas. Words matter; they can inspire or threaten. The power of discourse in a world where the mic is always on highlights the need to prepare for spontaneity and use the techniques set forth in this book.

Be intent on leading—always leading. See every situation as a potential leadership moment. But beware: Not every encounter is programmed for success. The guidelines in this chapter allow you to access the potential of a leadership moment. Run through that checklist, and if the stars are in alignment—go for it.

4 Be a Listener

The Stoic philosopher Epictetus observed, "We have two ears and one mouth so we can listen twice as much as we speak."[1] That's a point well made. Anyone who wants to excel in impromptu exchanges has to recognize that listening is an empowering process. It draws us closer to our audience. It allows us to hone our comments—and it lets us know how our remarks have been received. A commitment to truly hearing others is an important part of the impromptu mind-set.

But active listening, which this chapter discusses, involves more than listening with our ears. It's a threefold approach that requires our entire being—our *physical, mental*, and *emotional* powers. Master the art of actively listening and you'll make the most of impromptu encounters.

Use Your Body—Listen Physically

The first level of listening is physical—but it's not just about receiving sensory information through your ears. Your entire body should be involved when you listen actively. Your body language says a lot about how you are relating to others—and it sends a message about whether or not you are listening to them.

I once worked with a client who came to me because he turned people off and I quickly saw in his body language why. His hands and arms were folded. His head and body were turned away. No facial muscles moved when he spoke or listened—he had no warmth. His entire

body said to others, "I don't care what you think. I am in charge." Indeed, he felt he had all the answers and others needed to listen to him. As he put it: "My role is to sit in judgment all day. I'm in meeting after meeting. People come to me with problems to be resolved. I have to make the decisions. I have to say 'yes' or 'no.'" He viewed himself as the source of all answers, and his body language showed his insularity.

Body language can make you a better or worse communicator. When I make eye contact with you, I hear you better. When I turn toward you, you see that I am more engaged. It's the same when I turn off my smartphone and signal that I won't be distracted. Good physical listening begins with body language that shows you are interested in others. Open your hands and arms and direct your gestures toward the person you are talking to. Turn your head and body toward that person. Warm up your voice, and be expressive. Look people in the eye, and even in a group meeting, always look at the speaker even if that person is not talking to you individually. Smile, nod, show rapport. Pausing before you respond is also important. It tells your audience: "I want to think about what you just said." All these physical behaviors say, "I care about you, I want to understand you, I want to listen to you." And they will encourage you to concentrate more on your audience and enable you to read others more clearly. They will also encourage the speaker to be more open with you.

Effective listening also involves reading the body language of those you're talking to. If someone is stooped over with eyes cast down, they're telling you that you are not reaching them. Or, if someone is picking up her smartphone, assume your words are falling on deaf ears. Look at people's body language and ask yourself, "Do they look as though they are listening?" If not, change your pace, voice, or messages. This is the beauty of impromptu. You can adjust!

Physical listening also involves creating the right physical atmosphere for your conversations. Companies today are increasingly

concerned about creating the best spaces for listening. Designer Jennifer Magnolfi notes that businesses now offer "a wide variety of rooms for group interaction. They have building blocks of space that are specific to either one-on-one interaction or small-group interaction or large interaction."[2] Many leaders are also taking advantage of open environments to make themselves more accessible. A great example is Jack Dorsey, the cofounder of Twitter and head of Square. In Square's new corporate offices he works standing up "in the dead center of the open-air floor plan" because, as Dorsey puts it, "I'm much more accessible this way. People come right up to me and ask me questions if they need to."[3] This new environment creates huge opportunities for impromptu conversations and good listening.

But beware of obstacles in your physical environment that can inhibit listening. The biggest one is the interruptions that come thick and fast in open-office environments. The average worker experiences 50 or 60 interruptions in an 8-hour day.[4] Such interruptions can put you on edge and make you less patient with others. And if you're having an intense conversation with an employee, you might have to suspend the discussion when another colleague comes along and asks for a minute of your time. In some instances, companies offer more private rooms for such exchanges.

Active physical listening also requires that you eliminate electronic distractions. It's easy to become obsessed with what's on the computer screen. According to a McKinsey Global Institute study, we spend 28 percent of our time on email. That's twice the time we spend on communicating and collaborating in face-to-face encounters.[5] Computer time not only cuts down the number of conversations, but it inhibits the quality of those conversations if you find yourself talking while looking at the screen. Cell phones are another distraction. According to Pew research, young adults with cell phones exchange an average of 110 text messages on a normal day.[6] Even if you only glance at your phone when you're in a meeting, it gives others the feeling that

you're not listening (and, let's face it, you're probably not!). So, tune out all the distractions in your physical environment.

In sum, listening physically involves open body language, creating the right setting, and eliminating electronic distractions. It's so much more than just opening your ears.

Use Your Head—Listen Mentally

Listening mentally is the second tier of listening and involves fully engaging your mind in what those around you are saying and probing and building upon their thinking. This aspect of listening involves creatively working with the ideas the other person or group has put forth.

The starting point of mental listening is attentiveness. How many times do we find ourselves in a meeting and catch ourselves thinking about the next meeting, the previous conversation, or what we plan to do when we get home from the office? In her book, *Mindful Leadership*, Maria Gonzalez writes that "People spend up to 50 percent of their time not thinking about the task at hand, even when they have been explicitly asked to pay attention."[7] Gonzalez explains: "The untrained mind has huge difficulty in concentrating on anything for more than a few seconds, let alone a couple of minutes at a time."[8] The answer according to the author is learning mindfulness—through meditation and other practices. We must discover how to be "in the moment" of the conversation.

How do you know when you have achieved this state? Your thoughts are one with those you're listening to. You don't mentally "disappear" from the conversation. You stay with the flow and think about what you are hearing. Loblaws, a supermarket chain with over two thousand stores in Canada, understands the importance of listening and having its employees stay current with the conversations. Executive Ian Gordon explains: "We're talking a lot in our organization

about the notion of being present and fully engaged in a meeting and avoiding distractions like your phone or your next meeting."

One way to stay attentive is to "track" the other person's thinking. Make a mental outline of their points or take notes. Note taking—whether it's a one-on-one meeting or a group session—will help keep your mind grounded in the discussion and show your audience that you value what is being shared. Richard Branson, founder of the Virgin Group, said: "Sometimes you'll have a business meeting and nobody takes notes, and you know nothing's going to get done—if there's a list of 15 or 20 decisions that need to be made from it then it's critical I think to make a note and get these things done." Branson continues: "Some people think 'It's beneath me to be taking notes, that's something a secretary should be doing.' But forget that. Write these things down."[9] And it's best to take notes by hand rather than on your computer. Research indicates that although you can write faster on the computer, when taking notes the pen can be mightier than the keyboard. When you take notes with a pen, you are forced to synthetize the material and you end up with a stronger conceptual understanding of it.[10]

Mental listening also involves probing, drawing out others, and eliciting their views. Paul Vallée, CEO of Pythian, put it well when he told me: "If there are better minds in the room concerning a subject, it's really important to say, 'Lorraine's in this room and she's worked on this project.' Or 'I'm interested in what Bill has to say.' It's not a strength to always be imposing your opinion on others. It takes a lot of grace to sit back and listen."

As others speak, by all means ask questions and help them build their case. For example, you might say, "I heard you say you want to go in a new direction. Why is this important to you?" "How did you come to this conclusion?" "What alternatives have you considered?" If the person's thoughts seem unfocused, offer to help reframe them. Ask, "Is your point that … ?" Mental listening consists of deliberate, purposeful,

intentional questions that elicit a more constructive dialogue. There may even be times when listening and probing are the sole purpose of a meeting. For example, if you are in a client meeting, your goal may be to learn what the client's goal is for the coming year.

As you're listening mentally, pick up on verbal cues. Listen for phrases like, "So what I'm saying is. . . ." Listen for proof points like "first," "second," and "third." If the person often says "um" and "ah" or uses hedging phrases like "sort of" and "maybe," it's a good chance their ideas are not fully baked. Strong verbs ("I believe," "I know") as opposed to weaker ones ("I think," "I guess"), suggest that the speaker is committed to the ideas. Finally, listen for the "holes" in what's being said: If the story changes as the speaker continues—or if crucial information is conspicuously absent—you'll be able to pick up on the gaps that may need filling in.

Mental listening at its best involves orchestrating a discussion and bringing coherence to disparate views. You don't have to be the organizer of the meeting to do this. You can do it simply by taking a leadership role, listening to the ideas generated, connecting the dots, and bringing higher-ground thinking that incorporates various viewpoints. Here's what this would sound like: "I see where Stephanie is coming from, and it's really in a way what James is saying. The two ideas mesh in that they both are suggesting we undertake this investment, but with caution." Or, "All of us in this room have one goal: to see this project get off to an excellent start. I suggest we do all the things we have discussed here today in this order. . . ."

This capacity to lead a group discussion by listening mentally and synthesizing the ideas put forward is a huge asset. Organizations look for this ability in their top people. A CEO told me that one of his team members was "having trouble leading dialogue in the audit committee. He is too easily beaten into a corner. His tone fades when making key points. He needs to learn to elicit debate, dialogue, and consensus. He needs to pull from others at the meeting relevant issues and help the group resolve them."

I asked, "What would success look like for him?"

The CEO replied, "He would initiate robust dialogue around agenda items. He would have intelligent, thoughtful questions for the group. He would be able to bring about consensus, buy-in to quarterly audit assessment. He would no longer think of himself as an 'expert' but would view himself as an intellectually capable synthesizer of ideas, leading the group to collaborative thinking and shared outcomes."

These are skills any leader needs in meetings. This probing with a purpose is the highest form of mental listening, because it involves integrative thinking, collaboration, and it leads to consensus and action.

Use Your Heart—Listen Emotionally

The third tier of listening involves *emotionally* connecting with others and not letting your own feelings get in the way of effective listening. This ability to empathize is often underrated by leaders, but their employees place a high value on it. In a global survey by *The Economist*, C-Suite executives most frequently cited technology and finance as the two areas where they sought to improve. Yet lower ranking employees thought emotional intelligence and leadership should be their bosses' highest priority for development.[11] Clearly, employees want their leaders to be more sensitive. The starting point of emotional listening is reinforcement—nodding your head, or saying "yes" and "I understand"—but it doesn't stop there. Show that you empathize by using phrases like, "I can see why you feel that way," or "That must have been a difficult decision for you." This encourages others to open up and share their feelings, not just their thoughts and ideas.

Emotional listening also involves reading the speaker's nonverbal cues. Study that person's face, listen to their tone of voice, examine their body language, and draw a conclusion about how they are feeling. Suppose you're in a meeting with your boss and he takes a phone

call with another executive. On the call he becomes anxious, his tone is combative, and when the call ends he is restless and distracted. If you miss these cues, your meeting may be pointless. Best to ask, "Should we adjourn and meet another time?" Doing so will show him that you've read him and even if he says, "No, let's continue," you've shown that you've listened *emotionally*. He might even share something of the conversation with you.

A positive example of emotional listening occurred in our company. At a management meeting there was a contentious issue that seemed to be resolved. But one individual had his arms crossed and his face hung down. Another member of the team saw this and said, "I don't think you're comfortable with this decision. We need to know that you are comfortable." That sparked a whole other conversation in which the same participants delved deeper into the issue in an effort to resolve it so that *every single person* was on the same side. In the end, the decision was better. Tip: when you're in a meeting, read the room and listen emotionally to make sure everyone is in agreement. Some people may not want to stall a decision, so they don't speak up. But their nonverbal signs show they aren't in agreement. So say, "Hey, wait a minute … I think Lynn may feel differently about this proposal." The outcome will likely be better and your act of leadership will be the reason.

There are also verbal cues that need to be read, and if you listen emotionally, you'll be able to interpret them quite easily. If an employee says, "I'm happy with that raise," you can assume she is. Or, "I support that decision," means you have an ally. But sometimes words need to be deconstructed to get behind the real emotion. For example, when someone says, "Whatever!" that person really means "I know you don't care how I feel." "With all due respect" usually means "Watch out. I'm going to show no regard for your position." Or, "I'll go with the flow" means "I don't like the decision, but I'm not going to fight it."

When you feel someone has not come forward with his or her true feelings—and it's important for you to understand those feelings—it's time to probe. Here are some excellent probing questions.

- "How are you feeling about this situation?"
- "Would you have preferred a different outcome?"
- "I sense you have a concern about this decision."
- "Can you tell me more?"
- "Are you happy with this project?"
- "Are there any issues I'm not aware of?"

Once you know how the other person feels, *respond*, don't *react*. It's so easy to react emotionally if we don't like what we hear. Just remember the words of Dr. Seuss in *The Lorax:* "UNLESS someone like you cares a whole awful lot, nothing is going to get better. It's not."[12]

Even when someone does or says something that offends you, rise above it and don't put your own emotions in gear—that simply creates more tension and backlash. Listen and try to understand what motivates the other person. A great example of such a sensitive response is reflected in the following story, told to me by a client, who is head of investing for a financial institution.

> One of my teammates quit. He was not performing very well, and I had issues with that. He came into the room and said, "I'm resigning!" How did I deal with that? I didn't want to react with anger, I didn't want to tell him I'd invested so much time in him—though I had—and I didn't want to get mad at him and say "I can't believe you're quitting." Instead, I made sure my emotions were under control. I asked him why he was resigning, and I responded to each reason—culture, workload, and so forth. Then I said I could understand how he felt, but I would have liked a different outcome. Nevertheless, I respected his courage and confidence. It was a win/win. I didn't make him feel badly. And

I got feedback from him that was constructive and will allow me to make things better in my organization.

This impromptu situation could have turned into a battle of wills. The topic was unsettling and it would have been tempting for the boss to let his emotions take over. Instead, he sought to understand the emotions behind what he was hearing. If someone is coming from an emotional place we have two choices: (1) we can meet them at that same level and then the conversation becomes a battleground; or (2) we can work toward common ground, as in this situation. By using the latter approach you will be reshaping a more constructive conversation and taking it to higher ground. In a group session, if emotions flare up, acknowledge them and say, "There's a lot of emotion in this room, but we shouldn't let it overpower our intellect and good judgment."

Listening is an intensely creative process, whether it's physical, mental, or emotional listening. The knowledge you need for leading in the moment resides, in part, in those around you. It's their thoughts, their observations, their suggestions, their fears, their goals, their passions that give rise to your response. People will never follow you unless they believe you understand them. So a leader's mind-set must involve the desire and ability to listen.

5 Be Authentic

In their book, *Credibility,* James Kouzes and Barry Posner argue that "credibility is the foundation of leadership." As they explain it, "People have to believe in their leaders before they will willingly follow them."[1]

The path to trust lies in authentic leadership—being honest and open in all your impromptu conversations. Authentic leaders build ties with their audiences on a very personal level, by sharing their presence, ideas, beliefs, feelings, vulnerabilities, and stories. Today's world of constant personal interaction is no place for "corporate speak," insincerity, falsehoods, or wooden delivery. People expect more and leaders can give more of themselves. There is no better way to project this authenticity than in impromptu conversations that are unfettered from the bonds of traditional organizational protocols.

What Is Authentic Leadership?

"Authenticity" is a much-touted term today. As Adam Grant writes in the *New York Times,* "We are in the Age of Authenticity, where 'be yourself' is the defining advice in life, love and career.... We want to live authentic lives, marry authentic partners, work for an authentic boss, vote for an authentic president."[2] And, of course, be authentic ourselves.

But what does it mean to be authentic? The Greek root of "authenticity" is *authentikos* meaning "original" or "genuine."[3]

We express our authenticity when we share what's inside us, what's genuine to us, what's original in us. Authenticity is not a state, it's an act of self-expression. As Rob Goffee and Gareth Jones argue in *Why Should Anyone Be Led by You?*, "Authenticity manifests itself in context and in relationships with others. It is never solely an attribute of individuals."[4] By sharing that unique essence, we express our authenticity.

What, then, is *authentic leadership*? It involves sharing the genuine qualities that define us. But it is more than that. It also requires embracing the values and deep beliefs that represent leadership at its best. Those qualities include the intent to lead and listen, and to respect the views and dignity of others. These are the qualities discussed in this "impromptu mind-set" section of the book. If someone is in a leadership role, but does not have these qualities—instead preferring to disgorge any thought that comes to mind—then that person may be expressing a true nature, but is not an authentic leader.

Where does that take us when it comes to impromptu conversations? Today's world of impromptu exchanges provides abundant opportunities for individuals to express their best personal qualities. The most successful leaders share what they know, believe, feel, and experience in such a way that they inspire others.

People today are hungry for this authentic leadership. That's because in today's flatter organizations, in the absence of traditional hierarchies and rules, people are looking for role models, for lessons to ponder, for truth as we see it within ourselves. And in these everyday conversations you have the opportunity to find and project your own authentic self and turn others into followers.

Strategies for Showing Authenticity

There are many ways to bring your authentic self forward. The following six will put your audience (and you) in touch with your true self.

First, share your presence. The starting point of projecting authenticity is to be present—really, really there. This is far more than simply making yourself available for a meeting—or standing in front of the person you're talking to, or glancing up from your smartphone as someone asks, "Do you have a minute?" It is about being "in the moment," being open to the conversation and aligned with the person or people you're talking to.

An authentic presence is reflected in your body language. If you pass someone in the hall and ask, "How's it going?" and don't stay around to listen for the answer, you are being inauthentic. But if you ask the same question, stop, look the other person in the eye, and wait for a reply, you are showing a genuine sincerity. Similarly, if you have your head down or appear distracted or frazzled when others are talking to you, your physical actions will convey that you are not really there in that conversation. Your authentic self is somewhere else—inaccessible to you and to your colleague.

If you are on a conference call and checking email while someone is presenting at the other end of the call, you're not being fully present. You may think others won't notice, but they will. They'll hear it in your tone. So be present.

Second, share your ideas. Authenticity also means having the courage to share your thinking. There are many reasons people may not do so. Some find it easy to parrot the words and ideas of others—thinking that if they echo others, nobody will challenge or disagree with them. Others may hold back because they feel "corporate speak" is safer than coming out with their own views. Still others may not actually know what they think. That's right, some organizations have allowed—even encouraged—people to avoid thinking, avoid having their own ideas. This is especially true in top-down organizations, where uniform thinking often prevails. Authentic ideas, in contrast, are original, bold ideas that come from within you. Leaders need to delve deep to find them.

Elon Musk, CEO of Tesla Motors, is a leader who thinks boldly and shares his thinking with employees, investors, the business community, and the public. Despite his naysayers, he has stayed true to his clear thinking and has proved the doubters wrong. As he said in an interview:

"They would say, 'Well, you couldn't possibly make that [electric] car work.' And then we made the car work. And then they'd say, 'Well nobody's going to buy it,' and then people bought it. And then we announced the Model S and so many people called BS on that. It was ridiculous. And yet actually we were able to bring it to market. And when we brought it to market they said, 'Well you're never going to be able to increase the volume.' And we did that. And they said, 'You'll never be able to make a profit.' And then we did that in Q1. So I'm hopeful that, hey, if you will observe it, there's a trend here."[5]

There is an exciting rhythm to this passage. The cadence of his thought is so powerful because beneath the words is Musk's conviction about his ideas and his confidence that he and his firm will prevail. The same belief in the power of your ideas is necessary whether you're selling a product, promoting a strategy, or guiding a direct report or a team. Ideas—*your* ideas—matter tremendously.

Third, share your beliefs and values. Authentic leaders inspire others with their beliefs and values. Bill Gates is such an authentic leader. Simon Sinek, in his book, *Start with Why*, compares Gates to Steve Ballmer, who followed Gates as CEO of Microsoft. Sinek says that while Ballmer displays enormous energy, Gates has a deeper charisma that emerges from the convictions he shares with his audiences. Although Gates may appear "shy and awkward" at first glance, "[people] hang on his every word.... Those who hear him take what he says and carry his words with them for weeks, months or years."[6] Gates is compelling, according to Sinek, because he is willing to be himself without hype, and share his beliefs with others.

To unearth your most deeply held beliefs, follow Rosabeth Moss Kanter's guidance in her book, *Evolve!*. She advises that you ask yourself,

"Do I feel strongly about the need for this? Am I convinced that this can be accomplished? Can I convey excitement when I talk about it? Am I willing to put my credibility on the line to promise action on it? Am I committed to seeing this through, over the long haul? Am I willing to make sacrifices to see that this gets done?"[7] These questions and your ability to say "yes" to them, will shape your communications in ways that make you an authentic and believable leader.

My colleague, James Ramsay, a senior associate in The Humphrey Group, told me that when he coaches clients, he is constantly bringing them back to the idea of what they believe. As he explains: "I ask people to create lists—write down the five things they believe in. And then I say, 'Let's explore each of these beliefs.' This is what gives an individual the ability to answer questions and to speak authentically off the cuff." This inner probing is important for all leaders, because your audience will be able to tell whether you believe in what you are saying. And if you don't, they won't.

Fourth, share your feelings. Authentic leaders share their feelings—and do so with sensitivity toward their audience.

If you announce a reorganization or employee layoff in a wooden manner, you and your firm will come across as unfeeling and insensitive. To show your authentic and caring self in such circumstances, begin by making the HR material your own—put it in your own words. When you meet with your team to make the announcement, don't sugarcoat the truth, but be sensitive. After explaining the decision, show appreciation for the departing employees and the contribution they have made.

But beware of overemoting. I was told of an executive who cried on stage—when discussing the inferior quality of the product his team was producing. The audience was not impressed. The response seemed out of proportion to the issue. His leadership was compromised because he did not appear to be sincere. Authenticity is a tough thing! You have to show emotion, but not get emotional to the point that people feel you're putting on a show.

An important way of sharing your feelings is to show your passion—for your work, for the accomplishments of your team, for great new ideas, for your vision, and for your people. Passion expressed with the right words is always inspiring. As one client told me, "I get a lot of feedback from people who appreciate how deeply passionate I am about my work."

But don't let that passion turn negative—venting at those who don't meet your expectations or don't share your passion. You need to filter those negative emotions. Steve Jobs, for all his strengths, admitted that he lacked that filter. "This is who I am, and you can't expect me to be someone I'm not," he replied when biographer Walter Isaacson asked him why he could be so hard on people.[8] Authentic leadership is more than just being "who you are." It involves showing positive, motivational passion and filtering out destructive feelings that might demotivate others.

Fifth, share your vulnerabilities. Authentic leaders are forthcoming about their strengths *and* weaknesses. Patrick Lencioni in *The Advantage* writes: "The kind of trust that is necessary to build a great team is what I call *vulnerability-based trust.* This is what happens when [team] members get to a point where they are completely comfortable being transparent, honest, and naked with one another, where they say and genuinely mean things like 'I screwed up,' 'I need help,' 'Your idea is better than mine,' 'I wish I could learn to do that as well as you do,' and even, 'I'm sorry.'"[9]

Be willing to share your vulnerabilities. There is, of course, a fine line between undercutting yourself as a leader and sharing your insecurities, inadequacies, or missteps. For example, if you get up in public to give a speech, and confide to the audience that you don't like public speaking—that undermines your leadership. But if you confide to a colleague that you've accepted a speaking opportunity because you want to work on your speaking skills—it has never come easily to you—that's sharing a vulnerability.

As an authentic leader, you should not be hesitant to admit to members of your team—or to others—your vulnerabilities. Jeff Bezos told Amazon's first investors: "I think there's a 70 percent chance you're going to lose all your money, so don't invest unless you can afford to lose."[10] Why that confession? Bezos founded the company in 1994 when online commerce was in its infancy, so he knew the company could fail and he was up front about sharing that.

Sharing your vulnerabilities will do three things. First, it will make others feel closer to you, because we all have hits and misses, and everybody can relate when they hear yours. Second, sharing your "warts-and-all" self will make you feel good, because you'll see that people still respect you and trust you. Third, by being forthcoming in this way, you'll be able to build a better team, because you'll see that you can't do it all alone.

Vulnerabilities come in all shapes and sizes. It may mean admitting that you don't have all the answers. Stuart Forman, CIO in Canadian global information technology company, CGI, told me: "I spoke at a training session for our new managers. There were 400 people in the audience. At one point in the Q&A I said, 'I love that question. I don't have the answer for you today, but let me think about it. And I'll get back to you.'" Forman explained: "This, to me, is part of being authentic. I used to be worried about what they'd throw at me. I learned that there's nothing wrong with saying you don't know."

Sixth, share your stories. Nothing will endear you more to an employer, boss, team, colleague, customer, or friend than an inspiring story about yourself.

Career stories about how you've dealt with challenges are good to have if you're going for a job interview. Employers are increasingly looking for such personal narratives. Tobi Lütke, CEO of e-commerce software maker Shopify, says, "Our hiring is almost completely built around just going through someone's life story, and we look for moments when they had to make important decisions, and we go deep

on those."[11] So if you're applying for a job, be prepared to tell your best career stories.

Audiences relate to stories about professional struggles as well as personal tales about our families. Jack Dorsey, CEO of Twitter and Square, told a group of students: "My parents were some of the first people on Twitter." He elaborated: "My mom thought it was the way to contact me and my family. She thought Twitter was SMS. She thought it was a private channel. So she … was actually yelling at my brothers and saying, 'Jack when are you coming home.' And then she realized, 'Oh, wait a minute, this is public.'" Everybody in the room had a good laugh, no doubt imagining their mothers doing that kind of thing.[12]

Stories that teach business lessons are also excellent. Senior Vice President Ian Gordon, who oversees all product lines in Canadian supermarket-chain Loblaws, often tells stories at "Let's Talk" events for groups of eight to ten employees. "They love stories," Gordon said. "And they really liked my story about working at Frito-Lay earlier in my career." Here's the story as he told it to me.

> Following university, I started out in business driving a Frito-Lay truck. I got up at 5:30 in the morning and worked until 8 o'clock every night. I worked closely with variety store owners, and talked to them about our products. We had a product called Tostitos (still do!). The marketing people at head office in Frito-Lay decided that every year they would do a promo on Tostitos. They figured that they could save money if they posted contest rules on the only empty space on the Tostitos package—the window showing the product. There was one problem: the customers could no longer see the Tostitos. As a result, every year when Marketing ran the contest, sales would plummet. The contest would end and sales would pick up again. The variety store owners saw the problem and told me about it, but head office didn't. I learned from that experience that you always should listen to your customers. In my job now, as SVP of Loblaws Brands, I always listen to our customers.

Everyone can become an authentic leader—but don't expect it to be easy. As Warren Bennis writes in his book, *On Becoming a Leader*, "If knowing yourself and being yourself were as easy to do as people talk about, there wouldn't be nearly so many people walking around in borrowed postures, spouting secondhand ideas, trying desperately to fit in rather than to stand out."[13] Dig deep and find that authentic leader within you. Share your presence, ideas, values, beliefs, feelings, and stories with your colleagues, teammates, and friends. Inspire them by being true to yourself. And find joy in knowing that this new world of leadership invites us to be warmer, more sharing individuals.

6 Be Focused

In December 1944 the German army surrounded the American 101st Airborne Division in the Belgian town of Bastogne. The Germans sent the besieged Americans a letter, explaining why they must surrender. The U.S. commander, Anthony McAuliffe, replied with one word, "NUTS!" The American officer, Colonel Joseph Harper, who delivered this statement to the Germans was equally succinct when the Germans asked him just what the message meant. Harper said, "In plain English? Go to hell." The Americans held on, and the German offensive, called the Battle of the Bulge, collapsed. Those few words had made the American position—and resolve—unmistakably clear. Great leaders show a single-minded focus.

Information Overload in the Internet Age

The need for focus is important today because everyone is on information overload and you'll lose your audience if you don't deliver clear, focused thinking. In *Brief,* communications expert Joseph McCormack writes, "In 2008, Americans consumed about 1.3 trillion hours of information outside of work, an average of almost 12 hours per person per day."[1] At work, the demands are even greater. This onslaught of content is not likely to disappear, because everyone has become not only a consumer of information, but also a purveyor of information. Facebook founder Mark Zuckerberg remarks: "Now everybody who has a Facebook account has a voice. They can publish a

status update, or they can put a link out there with content they think their friends should read."[2]

Given this flood of information, it's no wonder people's attention span has gotten shorter and shorter. According to the National Center for Biotechnology Information, the average attention span of a human being has dropped from twelve seconds in the year 2000 to eight seconds in 2013.[3] This apparently is one second less than the attention span of a goldfish![4] Our short attention span creates a huge challenge for impromptu speakers, who have to draw their audiences back from distraction every eight seconds.

But that's not all. The sea of data that engulfs our audience's minds also invades our own mental space when we speak, making it difficult for us to focus. How many times a day do we hear speakers talking endlessly without knowing what point they're making? A client told me of a direct report who "couldn't say 'good morning' in less than 20 minutes." When we're verbose, others cringe when we approach them or talk to them.

Focusing and the Art of Impromptu

As a communications coach, I have worked with thousands of leaders over the past thirty years, and I've seen that those speaking off the cuff need greater focus. One of the most challenging situations I've had was working with a director who was sent to me because—in the words of his boss—"He's a big talker and he's driving me crazy because he talks and talks and talks, and never gets to the point." His boss said, "Can you make Cal pithy?"

This was an exciting challenge for me, so I said, "Sure."

When I had my first session with Cal I discovered how ingrained his loquaciousness was. Maybe it was genetic. His dad's nickname was "The Rambler." I worked with him and had him deliver a message again and

again, each time shortening it. We'd go through at least five iterations of one passage.

Finally Cal got to the point where he *was* pithy. In fact, he became the "poster boy" for succinctness. In meetings his boss would point out how short and focused his comments were. I was thrilled to hear this, and Cal was proud of his progress. But when I went to his boss to talk about the strides he had made, the boss said, "You know, Cal has one additional problem. He has such a compelling need to talk that when he was with our CEO recently he delivered 10 pithy messages in one conversation without stopping."

In a *Harvard Business Review* essay, psychiatrist Mark Goulston explains that many people feel compelled to speak incessantly, even when they have nothing to say. They do this, writes Goulston, for two reasons. "First, [for] the very simple reason that all human beings have a hunger to be listened to. But second, because the process of talking about ourselves releases dopamine, the pleasure hormone. One of the reasons gabby people keep gabbing is because they become addicted to that pleasure."[5] Talkers get a high from talking.

Besides enjoying the sheer pleasure of talking, many speakers don't focus because they *never ask themselves what their point is*. They organize their conversation around content. And given the fact that content can represent an endless stream of information, speakers can go on and on in content mode, without ever focusing their thinking and without ever coming to a point. I once had a client who wanted to have a town hall for his team. When I asked him what he intended to say, he answered with the following content dump:

"Off the top of my head I probably would go in there and talk about two or three things. What I want to focus on is basically a little bit of the year in review. And some of the accomplishments that we've had. And some preliminary thoughts on looking forward into the next year. And then I would have a list or chart of things. I'd say, 'Here are the great things we've done,' and I'd probably look at some

subcategories like client satisfaction. And I would probably try to pick another subcategory like technology innovation, or something a little sexier for the group. And I would try to pick examples that apply to my different business groups. And I might conclude by talking about some of the feedback and challenges we've had that would be a weakness next year."

This stream-of-consciousness approach to organizing one's thoughts is very typical. Many team leaders I've worked with begin with a big subject, then divide it, then divide those lesser subjects, and introduce charts, and in the end, all they have is an information dump. There is no argument. And this team leader ends on a negative note—"weakness next year." Just imagine this speaker with his haystack of content forcing his audience to search for a point (that proverbial "needle" in the haystack). Or, more likely, the audience would not bother searching for that point, tuning out instead.

This same content-driven approach is found in impromptu conversations when someone might ask a leader, "What's going on with your team?" and the answer will be a long laundry list of things that are happening. Or a boss might ask an employee, "Where do we stand on that project?" and the response would be an information dump about what's been done, who did what, and where it's going. This lack of a controlling idea is why so many people say as they conclude, "So my point is," or "I guess what I am saying is," or "to be clear." They only discover what they're trying to say at the end ... if at all.

A tip-off that someone is not focused is the use of filler words like "um," "you know," "I mean," and "well, it seems to me," while they are figuring out what to say. Even the brightest, most seasoned leaders fall prey to this tendency. One highly regarded CEO was asked about his company's plans for a certain technology and here is what he said: "I think the likelihood that Artificial Intelligence has a broad reach I don't know ... it's tough to say ... uh ... I think that's an interesting

question ... uh ... it could be a key area, but what we'll do remains to be seen ... we have people working on it. Time will tell."[6]

The solution? Have a focused mind-set that (1) encourages you not to talk, talk, and talk because you like to hear the sound of your own voice, and (2) distills your thinking rather than offering up a content dump. John F. Kennedy was a master of the focused comment. As Theodore Sorensen wrote in his book, *Kennedy*, "His answers were almost always brief. Some of the best were no more than a sentence or even a word. Would he comment on the possibilities of a neutron bomb? 'No.' Was he certain the Soviets really put two men in orbit? 'Yes.'"[7] Steve Jobs also distilled his presentations down to one message. "Today Apple is going to reinvent the phone, and here it is," he told his MacWorld 2007 fans.

Heed the words of Winston Churchill who had some fun with unfocused speakers when he said: "Before they get up, they do not know what they are going to say; when they are speaking, they do not know what they are saying; and when they have sat down, they do not know what they have said."[8]

In impromptu speaking, being focused is a make-or-break quality. You'll lose your audience if you speak too long or get sidetracked. But if you stay focused you can rivet your listeners' attention on exactly what you want them to know and care about. The power of leading in the moment depends on this ability to keep your audience focused.

7 Be Respectful

Daniel Craig, the 47-year-old actor who portrayed James Bond for nearly a decade, had just finished filming *Spectre*, his fourth Bond movie and the twenty-fourth in the franchise. He had one more Bond film to do—according to the terms of his contract—but he had been offered a new role in a TV series. When a reporter asked Craig if he thought he'd ever play Bond again, he declared, "I'd rather break this glass and slash my wrists. . . . All I want to do is move on."[1]

Aware that he'd insulted the Bond franchise, Craig did some quick damage control and the studio didn't fire him. But the fact that such a seasoned actor would veer off course and slam the role he'd been playing shows how careful we have to be when speaking spontaneously. Imagine an employee announcing publicly, "I'd rather slash my wrists than stay in this job another year! All I want to do is move on."

Today people speak off the cuff in ways that sometimes show disrespect for their organization and their colleagues. This habit may well derive from four emerging realities. First, people go "off script" more than they once did. The older approach of delivering vetted scripts was safer. Second, social media has amplified our voices, giving the angry or disgruntled a platform that not long ago did not exist. Bad news, whether broadcast in YouTube clips or tweets, seems to spread more rapidly than positive stories. Such irreverence and antagonism has become, for many, a cultural norm. Third, people change jobs more frequently, and may feel less affection for their organization. The concept

of lifetime loyalty stands as a distant memory. Fourth, stories of illegal and unethical practices have given rise to increasing cynicism toward corporations and governments.

While for some people showing disrespect may be an easy and tempting response, it is to be avoided. "Blowing off steam" may feel good in the moment, but it will look bad, and can damage reputations and careers. Speaking honestly and being open does not mean saying whatever comes into your head. As impromptu speaking becomes more common, and as hierarchies and organizational lines blur, everyone needs to be conscious of respect.

Respect Your Organization

True leaders show the utmost respect for their employer. If that sounds "old school," just think of organizations as *communities*. And as James Kouzes and Barry Posner point out in their book, *Credibility,* "Strong communities, and strong and vibrant organizations, only exist when people are willing to dedicate themselves to building something greater than themselves."[2] So loyalty to your organization shows your commitment to something larger than yourself. It shows you value a community that includes you, your team, your colleagues, your customers, and other stakeholders. As a leader, you should inspire others to believe in the organization and what it stands for.

Showing respect for your organization can take many forms. You convey respect when you share something positive or exciting about your company. It might be an inspiring chat with your team about the company's future, or a passing word with a staff member about a new maternity benefit the firm has just introduced. The hallmark of these exchanges is that they are honest, open, spontaneous conversations that elevate the business's reputation. Such communications are the lifeblood of any organization.

Still, disrespect happens far too often. It comes up in job interviews when applicants are asked why they left their last employer. If you say, "There was not much opportunity for personal growth within the company," the interviewer might wonder if it's only a matter of time before you direct your criticism toward the new firm. You're better off saying, "I had a great experience at the firm, but I feel it's time to move on to a position like this one."

Maligning one's firm can also take the form of grousing about not getting a promotion, a raise, a project, or a client. At such times it's easy to let down one's guard and complain. But statements like this chip away at a company's reputation. And that hurts, not only when the dialogue is among employees, but when outsiders hear comments from disgruntled employees.

Unguarded online conversations can be equally damaging to a company. Social media is not a place to share complaints. I recently saw someone tweet that he had worked in "soul-destroying Pharma. There's A LOT wrong with that industry." He may find that future employers or clients see that reference and dismiss him. Once an employee writes something critical about a company, that message is out there. Even if it's done anonymously, hackers can reveal a person's identity. It's always better to help position your firm positively.

Respect Your Management

When speaking off the cuff avoid comments that show disrespect for your boss or senior management. Organizations may be flatter than they once were, but showing respect is still a coveted quality. A *New York Times* article about Mic, an online news source created by and for millennials, highlighted a gaffe made by one of the younger employees.[3] CEO Chris Altchek had just responded favorably to a request that Muslim holidays be included in Mic's flexible time-off policy.

"Being inclusive and respectful of all religious affiliates is incredibly important to Mic," Altchek told the *Times*. But that statement wasn't enough for one staffer. In a small group meeting she told Altchek there were two words missing from his response to the request.

"What were those?" he asked.

"'I'm sorry,'" she said. "I didn't hear an apology."

This accusation that her boss failed to say he was sorry, delivered in front of a group, shows the dangers of pure spontaneity without respect for others. That staffer is no longer with the company. As corporate cultures become more relaxed and exchanges more spontaneous, there's still a need for sensitivity.

When I think of what respect for management looks like, I think of Mary Hundt, a senior HR business partner manager at BlackBerry. She has been with the company for decades, and openly admits that BlackBerry has its challenges. But she also respects what CEO John Chen and his senior management team are doing to turn the company around. She says, "We are trusting our leaders to take us through this turnaround. Anyone who is not trusting our leaders is going to take that negative message all the way down. And that's harmful to morale."

Does respect for senior management mean "kissing up" to your superiors? Not at all. The best employees are not subservient—they engage constructively with their superiors. That doesn't mean vehemently disagreeing or leveling criticism at your boss—a sure-fire route to shortening your time at a company. But it does mean speaking up, suggesting new ideas, and making recommendations that support the company and your boss's goals. Importantly, it also means understanding that those ideas may not always be adopted. When leaders support their senior management, they show respect and encourage others "all the way down" to do so. That makes for a stronger, more unified organization.

Respect Your Colleagues

Successful leaders are team players, and that means speaking and acting respectfully toward team members, colleagues, and associates. Respectful people are the ones who listen attentively to others at meetings, who don't interrupt when someone else is talking, who can be trusted with confidential information, and who always are generous and positive in their comments about others. They make others look and feel good.

I once had a client who came for coaching because she often found herself in combative conversations with her colleagues across the company. She said they got their backs up because—as she put it—"I have to bust into their organizations and they're threatened. I feel like saying, 'Hey, suck it up! That's life.'" She found it tough to show them respect. But we worked together to rethink her impromptu scripts so that she spoke to her colleagues' agendas—not her own—and she used more collaborative language. In today's business organizations, you need to lead across your organization, and if you want others to work with and follow you, you'll have to show them respect.

Leaders can also be challenged by the need to show respect to their direct reports. Some bosses can be difficult—raising their voices, accusing others of mistakes or shortcomings. That's a poor way of leading in the moment. Disrespect for direct reports can also be shown by not trusting them, not delegating enough. A vice president of a large multinational going through a restructuring sat down with his direct reports and told them: "Over to you. Have a chat. Decide on the best way to downsize our organization. And if you don't, I'll figure it out for you." Essentially the boss is saying he's not sure he can trust his team to come up with the answers. So he'll do it if they can't. He's not only threatening them; he's disrespecting them.

Be respectful, too, toward colleagues even when you are beyond company walls. Let's say you're having drinks after work, and the

conversation turns to people in your firm, and likes and dislikes about colleagues. Any criticism of a colleague or slurs of any kind will dilute the professional identity of the speaker. If you want to be seen as a leader shun such comments. You can even see these as leadership moments and say "let's not go there," or mention something you like about the person being slighted.

It's increasingly important, too, that in our diverse working environments everyone should adopt an inclusive mind-set that respects people of all backgrounds. Getting a laugh at someone's expense or pandering (even humorously) to stereotypes, puts one on dangerous terrain. And calling a room full of employees "you guys" when women are present is not considerate. It's time to retire stereotypes and show respect for everyone.

What can you as a leader do to reinforce respect among colleagues and team members? You can set a standard. A number of years ago, the board of a chronically underperforming Canadian forest products company brought in a new, change-oriented CEO to shake up its culture and improve results. He stressed respect as a key value and let it be known that there would be zero tolerance for gossiping about or talking down fellow workers behind their backs. It was amazing what a powerful cultural impact this guidance had. As one former employee put it, "It automatically made you feel more secure and more a part of an ethical, responsible organization."

Respect Yourself

Successful leaders also project a consistently positive and credible "brand" for themselves. They don't undercut themselves when they feel vulnerable, tired, or upset. Yet we hear people undermining themselves. Such self-inflicted wounds hurt their image and reputation.

Often when I speak I'll ask volunteers from the audience to come to the front of the room and receive coaching. One woman volunteered

to do so, and in front of an audience of 200 she practiced giving an impromptu elevator talk to her chief financial officer. It took great courage to do so, and we all applauded her. But her thirty-second pitch was filled with self-deprecation. Here's what she said: "Hi Rob. I'm Karen. You probably don't remember me but I was at the Finance breakfast the other day. I don't know if you realize it, but this was an eye opener for us. We in Legal were in the dark about the connection between Finance's goals and ours. But that's no longer true. So I'm happy we attended that event."

In a conversation that was supposed to positively position her in the eyes of her CFO, she implied that (1) she had no last name (always introduce yourself with first and last names); (2) she was not memorable, and (3) her group was "in the dark" before the session. None of these negatives was necessary. On her second take, she greatly improved and came across as much more confident.

Respect needs to be at the core of our impromptu conversations—and for that to happen we must make it part of our mind-set. Respectful individuals come across as having an impressive, positive style. Grace Palombo, EVP and chief HR officer of Canadian insurer, Great-West Life, told me, "There are a few executives who have shown me by their example how to speak well. Even when they deliver tough messages, there is an elegance and a graciousness to their style. What's so impressive is that there is a level of kindness in the way they speak." This polished style is not something one can "put on." It reflects the respectfulness that is at the heart of a leader's identity.

Your office provides an excellent place to learn and practice respect, because as leaders we have a responsibility to make organizations and the people we work with stronger and more capable. To inspire others and get them on side, you need more than impressive ideas. You also must show them respect and acknowledge their concerns. Do so, and you'll have an audience that listens and is eager to follow your lead.

Part III
The Leader's Script

8 Lay the Groundwork

In April 2016, just months after Justin Trudeau had been sworn in as Canada's twenty-third prime minister, he visited the Perimeter Institute for Theoretical Physics in Waterloo, Ontario, to announce $50 million in funding. After touring the facilities, Trudeau held a press conference, and a journalist jokingly asked him to explain quantum computing. To everyone's amazement, Trudeau launched into a clear and concise explanation.[1]

His words went viral and stunned even his admirers because, as *Vanity Fair* put it, "Man of Your Dreams Justin Trudeau Casually Drops Quantum Computing Lecture in Press Conference."[2] Why the accolades? Quite simply, because he had prepared extraordinarily well by mastering a highly technical subject. Doing so gave him credibility.

The six chapters that make up this section of the book discuss how to craft scripts for impromptu speaking. This chapter explores why preparation has been a fundamental for great impromptu speakers over the centuries. It also discusses the importance of knowing your subject and having a storehouse of key messages. In short, you will learn how to create a strong foundation for your script.

Great Speakers Prepare for Impromptu

When the term "off the cuff" first appeared in print in 1936, it already denoted preparation. It referred to the practice of writing notes on the cuffs of shirt sleeves and reading from these notes when speaking. Politicians, actors, and poets had long used this approach to write their scripts on what were then disposable paper cuffs.[3]

While people no longer write their notes on their shirt cuffs, the best speakers historically have taken time to prepare their extemporaneous remarks.

Demosthenes, the great fourth-century BC Athenian orator, was often called upon to address the Assembly. He would not speak until he had thought about the question under discussion. He explained that while he did not write out his remarks word for word, he believed that the speaker who prepares is the true democrat because formulating one's thoughts shows respect for an audience.[4]

Mark Twain too believed strongly in preparing his impromptu remarks. In 1879 he spoke at a meeting of the Society of the Army of the Tennessee, saying: "I have not listened to a bad speech to-night, and I don't propose to be the one to furnish you with one; and I would, if I had time and permission, go on and make an excellent speech. But I never was happy, never could make a good impromptu speech without several hours to prepare it."[5]

Winston Churchill also believed in the value of preparing impromptu remarks. In one famous instance, he paused before exiting his car as his driver opened the door for him just outside a building where he was to give a speech.

"We're here, Governor," his driver said.

"Please wait a moment," replied Churchill. "I'm still going over my 'extemporaneous' remarks."[6]

President Harry Truman learned the power of preparation when he spoke from bullet points while running for office in 1948. Unlike

most of his predecessors, he shunned formal campaign speeches, but he realized the need to prepare even though he wanted to sound more spontaneous. He won the nation over, and became so passionate that those who heard him would shout, "Give 'em Hell, Harry."[7]

Today when we see actors delivering acceptance speeches on Oscar night, we know many have prepared for their impromptu remarks, because they are much more eloquent than they would be if they were winging it. Some even have crinkled up notes in their hands.

Business leaders like Steve Jobs similarly create notes for impromptu remarks. In *The Presentation Secrets of Steve Jobs,* Carmine Gallo observes that "Practice allows [Jobs] to work largely without a script. During [product] demonstrations, Jobs conceals notes discreetly from the audience, but never reads them word for word."[8]

Today business leaders get the best results when they prepare their impromptu comments to teams, clients, or others. A young up-and-coming banker told me she was at an industry conference in London, England, and saw an opportunity with a few prospective clients. "So I stepped away from the conference," she said, "and I spent the break working on a brief pitch. I jotted down a few notes on the back of a business card, and burned the outline into my mind. And it worked. We have two new major European accounts."

While each of these speakers conveyed the *appearance* of spontaneity, they took a disciplined approach and developed some kind of script. Whether you have three weeks, three days, three minutes, or three seconds to prepare, use the time to organize your thoughts so you convey leadership.

Paul Vallée, CEO of Pythian, put it well when he said: "Winging it is appropriate only when you actually know what you are talking about and you are completely prepared for the conversation. Embarrassing yourself when winging it is easy. All you have to do is spout off about something you don't understand."

Indeed, reputations can be sullied by unprepared remarks. Clint Eastwood knows that. He spoke at the Republican National Convention in 2012 and it wasn't pretty! In an impromptu skit he talked to an empty chair, pretending President Obama sat there. Not only did he look a bit crazy, but he got his numbers wrong, and was off color. "I can't tell Obama to do *that* to himself," he said to a cringing crowd. Years after this stunt, Clint Eastwood said what troubles him most [in life] is "when I did that silly thing." That's a big price to pay for an ad-lib.[9]

Prepare well and you'll look good and avoid embarrassment. You don't have to be on a large stage as Clint Eastwood was, nor facing the media or a large gathering of your employees. Every time you speak you have a potential leadership moment, and taking time to prepare will enable you to maximize the impact of that opportunity.

The Starting Point: Know Your Stuff

The first step in preparing your extemporaneous script is knowing your subject matter. If you're giving a formal speech or PowerPoint presentation, this knowledge is embedded in your written remarks. But when speaking off the cuff, you need that content in your head, and that includes three kinds of knowledge.

Subject knowledge. People expect you to demonstrate a solid grounding on the topics you're discussing. If you are running a hedge fund, for example, you need to know what your fund is doing at any given time, what's happening in the industry, what the future outlook is, as well as the trend lines for historical data. This information changes daily, hourly—even minute by minute. Whether you're speaking in a meeting, in a corridor, over lunch, or at an industry conference, you need to be up to date on your knowledge.

Get your facts right, or risk damaging your credibility. A client told me that he still remembers a moment when his sales rep hurt

an important relationship because he got his facts wrong. "We were in front of a big customer, and the sales rep gave totally wrong stats. I knew they were wrong, the customer knew they were wrong, and we didn't look good." This same executive said, "In impromptu situations people often let their passion take over and their memory plays havoc with the facts. Or they never learned the facts in the first place." This is dangerous because your audience expects accuracy. Some of the most impressive political figures today are those who in media interviews are well-versed in their topic and speak with eloquence and grace about constitutional issues, legislative decisions, and the impact of policies on their constituents. In listening to them, one has the highest esteem for their depth of knowledge.

General knowledge. The better read you are, and the more you keep up with developments in science, politics, and sports, the richer your remarks and the more persuasive you'll be. Not everyone can emulate Trudeau in his knowledge of quantum computing, but a broad foundation of knowledge will allow you to respond to new circumstances, and draw upon the wisdom of others. Later in this book you'll read the remarks of Robert Kennedy upon the death of Martin Luther King. In this impromptu speech, Kennedy quoted the eloquent words of the Greek poet Aeschylus—lines that he knew well. That added depth to his moving tribute. If you have a favorite poet or writer, draw from that source to elevate your speaking.

Experiential knowledge. The best impromptu speakers also draw upon their life experiences. Martin Luther King's "I Have a Dream" speech was largely extemporaneous, but it embodied ideas he had lived. As Kathleen Hall Jamieson writes, "The eloquence of that speech flows from King's command of a rich rhetorical tradition, from his ability to voice his own and his people's convictions, and from his unremitting struggle to enable his audiences to witness the world as he had come to experience it."[10]

Our storehouse of experiential knowledge helps when discussing challenges in business. As Grace Palombo, a seasoned HR executive, told me: "There's a level of preparedness you need when speaking impromptu. After 30 years, I find issues arise that are similar to the ones I've faced in the past. So when a situation arises to which there is no obvious solution, I look for past scenarios that are similar, and think about how I have handled them."

So the starting point of preparation for impromptu speaking is making sure you have a solid grounding in your subject—as well as a broad base of knowledge drawn from many fields and your experience.

Keep Leadership Messages in Mind

Preparing for impromptu speaking also means having key leadership messages in mind. Mark Zuckerberg does this well. He is always "on message." His central message and mission is this: "To give people the power to share and make the world more open and connected."[11] He consistently delivers variations on this theme. Here are examples from his interviews and speeches:

- "I built the first version of Facebook because it's something that my friends and I wanted to use at Harvard ... a way to connect with the other people around us."

- "We stand for connecting every person—for a global community, for bringing people together, for giving all people a voice, for a free flow of ideas and culture across nations."

- "Connectivity will give everyone ... access to all of the opportunities of the internet."

- "Our 10-year roadmap is focused on building the technology to give everyone in the world the power to share anything they want with anyone."

- "Now really everyone who has a Facebook account has a voice."[12]

How does Zuckerberg achieve this consistency in his messages? By thinking about them and talking to others about them.[13] That's exactly how any leader develops a storehouse of key messages. By doing so you will be able to elevate your impromptu leadership conversations with messages that are consistent, clear, and compelling.

As founder of The Humphrey Group, I carry around a set of interlocking messages in my mind. The primary one is that we teach leadership communications. Every other message supports that key statement. For example, we tell clients we'll help them "lead every time they speak" and "lead up, down, and across the organization through strong communications." Our website announces: "Our sole focus is to help our clients lead in every communication." And this book is subtitled *Leading in the Moment*.

If leaders successfully articulate their key messages, everyone who works in their organization will think and speak with these same messages in mind. That's why I was particularly excited to receive a note from a new employee who wrote: "I feel very privileged to be a part of this company and support the vision you crafted more than 25 years ago, which is to instill in leaders that every communication is an opportunity to influence and inspire." This is the power of key messages: they become motivational for all whose lives they touch.

Whatever your organization, or team, or mission, write down your key message and supporting messages. Burn them in your mind, so you can draw upon them every time you speak. They will be the foundation of your many impromptu scripts.

These steps will help get you ready for impromptu situations. All good impromptu speakers prepare in advance, develop a strong knowledge base, and keep key messages in mind. As one client explained, "The best impromptu situations are when I'm overprepared. When I go in knowing my material cold, you could put me in any situation and I can pull from within my head what I need to get across."

9 Read Your Audience

I constantly have two tracks running in my mind. One plays what I am thinking and the other plays what I believe my audience wants or needs or expects from me. Half of my thought process is dedicated to my own agenda. The other half is in a place of empathy with my audience.

This insight, shared by Paul Vallée, CEO of global IT services company Pythian, shows the importance of reading your audience at the same time you are collecting your own thoughts. These "two tracks" must be constantly playing in our minds if we are to deliver the right messages in the right way. But reading your audience doesn't just take place when you're speaking. It needs to happen before, during, and after your conversation.

Reading Your Audience—In Advance

Take time to analyze your audience before you're face to face. Stuart Forman, CIO of CGI, a Canadian global information technology company, explained to me, "I tell my people, 'You have to get yourself into the heads of your audience. You have to know what's troubling them, what's working for them, what's not working for them, and what their hot buttons are.'" Knowing your audience will enable you to reach them. So ask yourself, "What is their appetite for the ideas

I will introduce?" "Will I need to bring them around to my way of thinking?" And "If so, what is my best strategy?"

Assessing your audience's level of knowledge is also critical. Will you need to explain the basics to them, or do they have a sophisticated knowledge of the subject? Adeola Adebayo, a principal at OMERS, one of Canada's largest pension funds, learned a lot about reading her audience from her boss. She told me that she was prepping for a conversation with a senior-level audience. She had a lot of expertise herself, but her boss said that she shouldn't assume senior management had the same technical knowledge. "Look at it this way," he said. "It's as though you have a Ph.D. in this subject, and your audience is in elementary school." "So that's how I prepared," she said. "I had some words I couldn't avoid—words like EBITDA, net debt, and covenant ratio. But I deconstructed them for my audience. I explained them in simple terms like 'the higher this number, the worse it is for us.' Or I'd show the metric in a chart, and explain when the line goes up, it's bad, and when it comes down, it's good."

Reading your audience in advance also will make you aware that there might be people with very different agendas. You will need to decide who your target audience is. It won't necessarily be the most senior person; it might be a colleague or client. Ask yourself, "Who in the group will I really be talking to? All of them equally? Some more than others?" You really have to think about who is important to the decision you are seeking. There is, of course, a danger in focusing on the boss, and not addressing the others in the room. Even if you want the boss's approval for your project, you need to spread your eye contact around so it's not too obvious that you have a one-person audience.

If you're targeting a single person, learn as much as you can about that individual. I heard a story about a business leader who did just that. He was invited to a dinner and studied the bio of the CEO who would be hosting the event. He approached the CEO during the

mix and mingling time, and said, "You're Phil, you're the founder of this company, aren't you?" He praised the CEO's accomplishments, and briefly mentioned a few of his career milestones. The CEO later told me, "The fact that my guest had bothered to get to know me in advance really made an impression on me. That level of preparation was amazing. After that meeting this person could call me up any time of the day or night and I would be happy to do anything for him."

Analyze your audience in advance and you'll know how to make the best case for your ideas. If you're a manager of compensation and have just gotten approval on a new plan, customize that message for each audience. When talking to your team, highlight the program's benefits to employees. If you're speaking to your supervisor, trumpet your success in getting the plan accepted. If you're talking to senior management, explain how the new program will attract and retain employees and build the talent pool of the firm. A clear understanding of your audience will shape everything you say.

Reading Your Audience—As You Speak

Once you're in front of your audience, be sensitive to the dynamics in the room and respond accordingly. When speaking, keep the following questions in mind and let them guide you in reading your audience.

Is my audience engaged? Carefully monitor the engagement and energy level of your audience to see if you are reaching them. Let's say you're making a pitch to a group of colleagues and you see that their attention is fading, change your approach. If you're talking to a client with a pitch book in front of you, and you see that the client is turning the pages and not listening, put the book away. Mary Vitug, a seasoned managing director in equity capital markets, told me, "I once worked with a mentor who would actually avoid the pitch book. His ability to gain the confidence of the client came from his saying,

'Look, we have a bunch of facts here in the book, but let me tell you why we think this deal works.' He walked away with a lot more business."

Observe the body language of those in the room. If you see members of your audience sitting back in their chairs—or fiddling with their phones—or slumping in their seats, or crossing their arms, change your approach, because you may be losing them. If on the other hand, their eyes are riveted on you, and their bodies are turned toward you, and their faces are animated, you can be pretty sure you're getting through to them.

Which ideas are gaining traction? Read the room and recognize which ideas are taking hold. Dr. Allan Conway, former dean of the University of Windsor's Odette School of Business, told me he monitors these dynamics every time he walks into a classroom: "I read the room and my approach to lecturing is shaped by the flow of ideas in the class. If I have something prepared, I'll almost always want to do something that's more spontaneous. A lot of it will depend on the students. Their involvement will signal to me what they see and don't see. Suddenly I'm responding to their insights and filling their gaps."

The same holds true in business meetings: Discover what your listeners are thinking and build upon the ideas they put forth. That way you'll have a more robust and collaborative discussion. For example, if you're making a pitch to a client, draw out that person's views. Ask if anything has changed since the last meeting. You'll get more buy-in from them if you build upon their current thinking. If you're monitoring the flow of ideas in the room you'll also want to watch for conflicts, and resolve those as best you can.

What is the organizational culture? Every organization has a culture that defines the way people interact. Cultures can be formal, informal, competitive, collaborative, family, or tribal. Be sensitive to the cultural dynamics that shape your impromptu interaction. Toni Ferrari, a vice president at TD Bank Group, is very attentive

to the cultural realities of her organization. She points out, "We're a very collaborative culture and it's not always a good thing to come across as the smartest person in the room or the only opinion at the table. It is important that you come across as having considered everyone's opinion to collectively come to the right decision. I make sure to ask if everybody has expressed their view before I make a recommendation."

On the other hand, if you're in a more competitive cultural environment, you'll do well to develop a thick skin and focus on presenting your ideas confidently, forcefully, and without trying to be nice to everyone. It's not that you want to hammer others, but you do want to hold your own, and this can mean challenging others, coming back when you've been challenged, and generally showing conviction and confidence in the way you speak. Knowing the cultural "rules" of your organization—or any group you're talking to—is critical to your success.

Be sensitive, too, to global cultural differences. If you are on a global conference call beware of idiomatic language. A vice president told me his boss delivered an impromptu motivational speech in Japan. He began, "We've got to put the pedal to the metal." And everybody looked confused. Then he went on, "We have to knock one out of the park," because he's a big baseball guy. They didn't get that either. My vice president friend had to spend the next afternoon explaining to his team what his boss meant.

What political realities are present? Even though organizations today are flatter than ever, there are still "tops" and "bottoms" and layers in between. Senior leaders need to be treated not with groveling behavior or obsequiousness, but with respect for the office they hold and the role they play in decision-making. This means acknowledging their views, listening carefully to their opinions, building upon what they say, and showing the appropriate deference. And when challenging them, do so in a way that is not confrontational. In fact, this is good protocol to apply when you're speaking to anyone.

Senior leaders, for their part, must also be aware of power dynamics and not upstage their team members. One vice president told me, "The fact that I am present may discourage people from expressing their own views. They may take what I say as the ultimate answer. So I will sometimes say to them, 'I'm brainstorming with you and I really want you to challenge me, and bring forward your ideas, because I don't have the answer.' You can empower others to lead. Or you can express your opinion on everything and discourage others from thinking."

How are male and female colleagues interacting? A final area for reading the room is gender dynamics. Women are interrupted far more often than men.[1] And women themselves often let their male colleagues take the stage, since men typically have stronger voices and more confidence about speaking up. My advice: rebalance the conversation. If someone is silent but you know she has a quick mind and is a key decision maker, ask for her opinion. If a few people are dominating the discussion, say you'd like to hear from those who have remained silent. Bring the room to life by engaging everyone.

Reading Your Audience—Afterward

Whether you've been pitching business, talking at a networking event, speaking to employees at a town hall, attending a job interview, or having a quick corridor conversation, follow up by asking yourself, "Did I 'get' the audience?" "Did I read the situation correctly?" Those postmortems are valuable and a good way to improve your skills.

A vice president I worked with told me that her boss encourages such reflectiveness not only after an important presentation, but after each encounter with a client. "So," she told me, "I began to ask my (internal) clients if I had understood their needs. But I ran into a snag when one client said, 'Well, you could add more value.' And he

started telling me how and why. I clearly had misread him. It came down to the way I was communicating with him. He showed me that I had been too quick to say, 'Well, you should do this, or do that.' I decided I would start listening to him. Six months later, I began to get really good feedback from him."

In sum, always think in stereo—one track keeping tabs on your own thinking while the other track monitors the audience's response. And to be a great impromptu speaker, read your audience—before, during, and after you speak.

10 The Scripting Template

Alcidamas, the fourth-century BC rhetorician, believed in the importance of impromptu speaking, and he argued in his treatise *On Composers of Written Speeches* that impromptu speaking requires much more skill than scripted speaking. "If one who spends his time writing [speeches] changes over to extempore speeches," he wrote, "he will have a mind full of helplessness, wandering and confusion."[1] For this reason, Alcidamas argued that we should prepare our impromptu remarks in advance by mentally structuring what we will say.[2]

Wise advice. Whether you're delivering your impromptu remarks tomorrow, an hour from now, or in five seconds, plan what you'll say. The degree to which you can do this will depend upon how much time you have. But in every situation it's important to collect your thoughts rather than spew out whatever comes into your head. Winging it simply doesn't work for leaders. It causes the "wandering" and "confusion" Alcidamas mentions.

This chapter introduces the Leader's Script® template, a model for organizing your thinking in impromptu conversations. It was developed by The Humphrey Group, and is used in all of our training.

The Leader's Script Template

This easy-to-master template has a four-part structure rooted in the fundamentals of persuasion.[3] The diagram below shows the elements of this template.

```
┌──────────────────────────────────────────────┐
│              The Leader's Script               │
│                                                │
│   Grabber:                                     │
│                                                │
│   Message:                                     │
│                                                │
│   Structure:                                   │
│   I.                                           │
│   II.                                          │
│   III.                                         │
│                                                │
│   Call to Action:                              │
└──────────────────────────────────────────────┘
```

Here's how it works:

- **First, Engage Your Audience with a "Grabber."** This bridge to your audience can be a friendly greeting, a reference to a previous discussion, or a segue from someone's point. Chapter 13 ("Beginnings and Endings") discusses the grabber.

- **Second, State Your Message.** This is your point. It is the heart of your impromptu script. Chapter 11 examines the role and attributes of a message.

- **Third, Build Your Structure.** Create a compelling case for your message with clear, persuasive arguments. See Chapter 12 for a discussion of structure.

- **Fourth, End with a Call to Action.** Show how your message can be acted upon. Chapter 13 explores the call to action.

This four-part template will allow you to lead others through persuasive and sound thinking. Burn it in your mind and use it every time you speak impromptu.

Illustrating the Template

So you probably want to know, "How do I actually use this model in the kind of situations I face?"

Suppose you are preparing for a job interview. Jot down the key elements in your script. You might begin with a grabber that offers up some gracious words about the interviewer, and your appreciation for being considered for the position. Next comes your message: say why you believe you're a strong candidate. Following the message, give several reasons you feel qualified for the position. Close with a call to action: Inquire about next steps and share your excitement about becoming the chosen candidate. These elements, if jotted down in advance and held in your mind, will provide cues for you in the actual interview.

Let's take another situation: you're about to meet with your boss for an update on a project. Take 10 minutes before the meeting to write down the key elements of your script. Your grabber might bridge to your boss by saying, "I know you're keenly interested in Project X." Your message would follow: "I've got good news: We're making excellent progress." Now for your proof: Jot down several points that illustrate why you say things are moving along well. Close with action: What do you want your boss to do? Or what will you do next?

That's it—a simple template that guides you through any discussion. If you take the time to jot down on paper or in your mind these four elements of an impromptu script, you'll sound scintillatingly spontaneous.

Using the Leader's Script

There is no more critical a skill for impromptu speaking than this ability to structure your thoughts. A manager once complained to me that no one listened to him. He told me: "My boss's boss was reading his emails the entire time I was speaking to him last week. He never looked up once. At other times when I'm talking to my boss, he asks off-the-wall questions, as though he is trying to throw me off." The reason no one listened to him was that he was making it very difficult for others to follow him because he put his material together in a helter-skelter fashion. He would come out of the starting gate with whatever was on his mind and there was no message or logical structure. Worse still, animosity was building up because he felt his boss was "trying to throw him off" when he was actually asking for clarification. This individual was a case study in the need for using the scripting template.

The Leader's Script has an important advantage: It encourages us to deliver more thoughtful remarks than we might if we just "let it happen." Let's say you are a manager and you say to one of your team members, "Good luck with that client presentation." You've expressed a positive sentiment, but little else. If you have the template in your mind, your comments will be far more enlightening. For example: (GRABBER) "I'll be anxious to hear how your presentation goes." (MESSAGE) "We have a golden opportunity to build a new relationship with this client." (STRUCTURE) "I know they're ready to choose a new provider and they want exactly what we have to offer." (CALL TO ACTION) "Make it happen!"

Delivering from the template takes discipline—whether you create the arguments in advance or on the spot. If you know you'll be speaking in an impromptu situation, prepare the skeleton of what you'll say by using the template. Then burn it in your mind. All you have to create on the spot are the words. As Virgin Group's Richard Branson advises:

"It helps to have a rough outline of where you're going to take a point, to keep the conversation moving forward."[4]

If you can't prepare in advance, you can still use the template. Build your outline as you speak. PAUSE and think of your grabber. Deliver your grabber. PAUSE and think of your message. Deliver your message. PAUSE and think of your structure. Deliver your structure. PAUSE and think of your call to action. Deliver your call to action. In short, pause before each element so you can create that next component. If you pause, you'll sound more confident and your script will be that much better.

Scalability of the Leader's Script

One of the great features of this template is that you can expand and contract it to fit the occasion and time frame. You can even shrink the number of elements when the occasion requires a quick response.

For a meeting comment, you might have only a grabber and message: (GRABBER) "I fully agree with you." (MESSAGE) "We need to be more collaborative." If you want to expand the script for a pitch to your team, add the structure and call to action. The structure might refer to ways of being more collaborative: (1) "We must trust each other." (2) "We need to share information and ideas with each other." (3) "And together we will build solutions that reflect this shared knowledge." The call to action could be, "Are we all in?" Let's say you want to turn this short script into a town hall talk. Make it still longer by expanding your structure and elaborating your call to action.

This scalability also allows you to deal with unforeseen circumstances. You may have planned to give a thirty-minute PowerPoint presentation, but your boss says, "I've got just five minutes," so you downsize it to your grabber, message, structure, and call to action—essentially an executive summary. If you're at a networking

event and see that the person you're talking to is restless, shorten your script. When you're in the elevator and the doors open for you, reduce your script to a message and call to action. ("I've got an idea I want to share with you—let's grab coffee.") If you are having a leisurely lunch with a client, you can prepare proof points about how you'd like to work with that company, but if your client just wants to chat, cut the proof points. The only rule is this: Be sure you always have a message.

Creating your script is an important aspect of impromptu speaking. It will keep you from blathering, as so many people do. With a clear and persuasive structure, you will influence and inspire your listeners. The next three chapters look more closely at the components of a script.

11 Commit to a Message

Does having a message make a difference? Absolutely! I once coached the head of sales for a large telecommunications firm. He was in the final stages of competing for a major contract—supplying an aerospace company with a communications system. The stakes were high—with hundreds of millions of dollars to be awarded to the winner. Competition was fierce.

After weeks of technical discussions, the aerospace firm asked each of the bidders one final question: "In ten words or less, why should we choose you?" Most of the suppliers couldn't answer the question. They fumbled, saying, "It's really impossible to state our value equation in so few words." They explained that with twenty-five components to the bid, it would take much longer to describe their offering.

But my client was ready with a message. He said: "We are the sole provider of peace of mind." He assured the executives they could sleep at night knowing that all the components would be in place and working well. That was what they needed to hear and they chose his company. That's the power of a single, clear, compelling message. At the heart of the Leader's Script is a point—your point. It is the idea you want to get across.

Why Have a Message?

I came across a funny but all-too-true cartoon recently in which a disgruntled boss was sitting behind a large desk shouting at a stressed-out employee. The caption revealed the boss's frustration: "You make a good argument, but I'm still missing the point."[1] The bottom line of speaking is to have a point, and make it clearly. You shouldn't expect your audience to know what you're saying if you don't know what you're saying.

Your message gives you a reason for speaking and others a reason for listening. As Mary Vitug, a managing director in a large financial institution, said in an interview for this book, "Demonstrating that you have a point of view is critical. There are lots of words exchanged in any meeting, so whoever delivers a clear message stands out."

Without a message, conversations become information-based rather than idea-based. Listeners are not sure what point you're suggesting or why you're proposing a certain action. Put bluntly, an update without a message wastes everyone's time. People who speak without a message have language filled with jargon, "corporate speak," and filler words. It's not the language that's the primary problem. It's the confused thinking behind the language. So be sure your side of the conversation always has a point. That way you're telling others, "Here's what I believe. Here's what I want you to buy into." Your listeners will appreciate your clarity.

The best leaders foster the sharing of ideas by encouraging others to express their views with strong, clear messages. Steve Jobs is a good example of such an executive. As one account notes: "The more mature and confident [Jobs] became, the more he surrounded himself with strong, opinionated executives who felt comfortable arguing with him."[2] Sundar Pichai, Google's CEO, similarly encourages the flow of ideas. In a half-hour meeting, according to a *Fast Company* article, he

and staffers discussed "the power of artificial intelligence, the value of integrating Google Photos with other products such as Google Drive, [and] the importance of creating an emotional bond with the users of an app." Pichai was enthusiastic and responsive. When the team showed him a rough cut of a promotional video, his response was a "heartfelt: 'That's awesome!'"[3] Compelling messages will create "aha" moments for the whole room. Without those messages, exchanges can get bogged down in operational, technical, or tactical concerns.

Simply put, leaders lead with messages. And these don't just come to mind in the moment you're speaking. You need to have "back pocket" messages: clear leadership thoughts stored in your mind, ready for any one of your impromptu conversations.

Characteristics of a Message

The best speakers know the qualities of a good message. With a bit of practice, you'll be able to embed these must-have qualities into all your impromptu messages. Here are the six characteristics to keep in mind.

First, a message is one idea. Streamline your thinking down to one essential idea—the point you want your audience to buy into. Keep that focus as you're speaking. Sometimes speakers have too many ideas ... or they have no idea what they're trying to say. Too many ideas—or no idea—both produce the same thing: confusion in the minds of the audience.

Second, it's a single, clear sentence. Why? Because if your message is more than one sentence, or is a long, convoluted sentence, the audience will not "get it." For example, if you say to a client, "We're here for you, we can deliver. And of course we want to work with you on this next opportunity, which sounds very exciting," you'll be leaving the client with multiple messages. A simpler, one-sentence client pitch

message might be: "We're confident we can deliver for you." In an internal meeting your single sentence message might be: "Let's explore that plan." Or, "To succeed as a team we need to work more collaboratively." Just think of the messages we've heard from well-known leaders. Jeff Bezos, for example, sums up the power of risk taking when he says, "That's actually a very liberating expectation, expecting to fail."[4]

Third, it is engaging. Your message should engage the hearts and minds of your listeners. You want your audience to buy into your main idea. Design it so your listeners hear it, believe it, and want to follow it. This means knowing what will move your audience. I once asked a director of strategy who had just joined a firm, "What would your message be if your boss asks you, 'How do you see your job?'" He replied, "I'd say, 'My goal is to get the company to live the strategy.'" That would have been music to the ears of the VP of strategy.

Fourth, it carries your convictions. Make sure your message is an idea you believe in. When Lou Gehrig got up in front of fans at Yankee Stadium to announce that he was ailing, he delivered a deeply felt message. He could have expressed regrets, but instead his message was, "I feel like the luckiest guy in the world." Don't undercut yourself or your company with half-hearted statements. One CEO told analysts, "I'm pleased to say we turned in some pretty decent numbers," when he could have said, "I'm delighted to announce that our performance this quarter was the best ever."

Fifth, it is positive. Your message should move the room, so be sure it embodies hope, aspirational goals, possibilities, and accomplishments. For example: "I'm thrilled by your performance as a team." Or "We closed the deal, and you all made it happen."

This doesn't mean you sugarcoat reality. You might have a message that begins with a negative and ends with a positive, like this: "While we face unprecedented challenges, I am confident we can remain the provider of choice in our industry." When there are both negative

and positive elements in your message, make sure the positive comes last—always move from negatives to positives. Or you can build a sense of urgency (or concern) in your audience, then move to your high-ground message.

Such was the approach of a forest industry CEO who needed to get management and the union at a sawmill to work together during a very challenging time for the industry. He got up in front of employees and said, "Some have urged me to dismantle this mill, put it on a barge, and reassemble it in China." He then told them—and this was his message—that he believed they could come up with a joint plan to make the mill succeed and he'd give them ninety days to do just that. And they did! That message—and the urgency behind it—drove a huge cultural shift that ensured the mill's survival.

Sixth, it's recognizable. Make sure everyone can identify your message when they hear it. Often expressing it as a strong, clear, declaratory statement (with a tone of conviction) is enough to flag it as your main idea. But if you want to ensure that your audience gets it as your message, begin it with words like, "My point is," "My message is," "My view is," "As I see it," "I believe that," or even "Here's the thing."

The Power of a Message: An Example

No single sentence in the Leader's Script has such power as your message. It changes the character of your remarks. It focuses your thinking, and lifts your audience to higher ground.

When you don't have a message, your listeners are left to sort through the details and figure out what you're trying to say. They may be frustrated by your lack of clarity. Here's an actual example—*sans* message. James, an operations director in an oil and gas company, is sharing bad news with his CEO, Glen. You can hear the CEO's frustration as he tries to puzzle out the situation.

JAMES: Glen, I'm here because we have a situation that's kind of out of the ordinary, and it's not one we're very happy about. The situation is that during the drilling of one of our wells, we unfortunately cemented the drill pipe in the hole. The well bore is junked and has to be abandoned. We need to redrill the well. We have 11 million dollars in the well, and that is money spent with no recoverable reserves.

The good news is that the last casing, which we set, is well positioned and we can get down to that point.

GLEN: How the hell did this happen?

JAMES: It was human error. Instead of putting 15 cases of cement down the hole, we put 70 cases down. We will do a full postmortem on it and will come back to you with a report.

This is a script without a message. No single sentence stands out as the defining idea. There's a lot of information, but no focused argument. And in the absence of a positive message, negativity takes over. Just look at the number of sentences that carry bad news. No wonder the CEO came forward with a "how the hell" interjection.

How might the speaker have delivered this news? What would a message-based script look like? The following reframes the script with an up-front message (in bold):

JAMES: Glen, do you have a moment? There's something I'd like to speak to you about urgently. **We've lost well #240, but we have a solution to the problem.**

We inadvertently put too much cement down the hole, and cemented the drill pipe into the hole. We've done our best to fix the situation over the past two days, and have come up with a solution. We can still use the good casing in it and drill a new hole from the bottom of the casing past the cemented drill pipe. We're ready to go. All we need is your agreement.

GLEN: Sure, let's get this thing fixed.

The revised message-based script does a number of things: It immediately alerts the CEO to the speaker's message. It is more focused and shorter. It is positive (the negative, defensive detail is gone). And it is well structured (with a grabber, message, structure, and call to action).

Message-based speaking allows you to lead, influence, and inspire by getting to your point early, and shaping your script around that idea. It makes you look a lot more confident and persuasive. We in The Humphrey Group have taught tens of thousands of leaders to speak with a message, and they often tell us how doing so has transformed their speaking immeasurably.

With practice, coming up with a message each and every time you speak spontaneously will become second nature to you. You'll *think message*. But developing your message can take courage—particularly if you're speaking upward in an organization. Realize that your listeners, even your superiors, want you to be clear. They want you to get to the point and not waste their time. Speaking with a message is a powerful strategy if you want to be heard in today's knowledge economy.

12 Make a Compelling Case

It was once said of Mark Twain that "he drew from the 'divine ragbag' of his mind whatever it offered and left it to the reader to discern the relevancies and sequences."[1] Twain was a creative genius and could get away with digressive narratives. But speakers who draw from the "ragbag" of their minds and let their listeners piece together the structure of their remarks risk losing their audience. Clear organization is fundamental, and the Leader's Script will enable you to make a compelling case every time you speak.

The Role of Structure

A sound structure does some heavy lifting for you: It allows you to get your message across. If you say to a colleague, "We need to work on our client pitch," and you don't explain why, the thought dangles. If you tell an employee, "I am confident you can lead this project," your listener will expect you to explain the reasons you believe that. Hence the need for proof points. Stating your message is rarely sufficient. You need evidence that encourages listeners to buy into that point of view. So after presenting *what* you believe, share *why* you believe it.

Structure your script in advance when you know you'll have to say a few words or field questions. But even when you have little warning,

create a set of bullet points—on paper or in your head—that support your argument.

Adeola Adebayo, a principal at OMERS, one of Canada's largest pension funds, told me she has to come up with proof points several times a day. Her boss might come to her in the hall and say, "I just read something in the news about Company X. I know you're following that sector. What do you think about this company?" She'll reply: "Yes, we invested in it and it's still a good investment." But she knows that just having this message is not enough. "My boss would expect proof," Adebayo explains. "So I'd say, 'There are several reasons Company X remains a good investment.'" She'd then provide bullet points:

- First of all, it's the largest company in its sector in our country.
- Second, it generates significant cash flows.
- Third, although it operates in a volatile industry, it has strong liquidity.
- Fourth, it has the support of the investment community and access to the capital markets.

She might conclude with the following call to action: "I suggest we increase our investment in Company X." This is a great example of how to respond in the moment with a cogent set of arguments. Sound simple? If you make it a habit, it will be.

Make sure your bullet points argue your case, and are not simply topics. Suppose Adebayo had responded to her boss's question with this answer: "There are three aspects of Company X that I've looked into: their financial results, their oil reserves, and their place in the industry." That approach would offer information but no conclusion. It makes no point. As a leader you need to speak with a structure that carries forward an idea.

Patterns of Organization

Building your case involves choosing the right pattern of organization for your points—and with impromptu speaking this choice often happens in the blink of an eye. The secret is to learn the following four patterns and pick the best one for each impromptu script.

1. **Reasons.** This pattern backs up your main point with reasons.

   Suppose your message is, "I believe we need a more inclusive working environment."
   Your bullet points might be:

   - First, we're way behind in hiring women and minorities.
   - Second, a diverse workforce leads to a better bottom line.
   - Third, inclusivity is the right thing to do!

2. **Ways.** This pattern shows the ways your main point can be acted upon. Or it can refer to "things" that have to be done.

   Suppose your message is, "I know we can fix this situation for our customer."
   Your bullet points would show the ways:

   - First, we will interview our customer.
   - Second, we'll assign a team to resolve the situation.
   - Third, we will follow through and make sure it's fixed.

3. **Situation/Response.** This pattern is used when your message refers to a situation or challenge to be acted upon. The first bullet describes the situation or challenge, while the second presents the response.

   Your message might be, "Although last year's results came in below expectations, we've taken steps to turn the division around."
   Your bullet points would sound like this:

   - Adverse economic conditions resulted in earnings that were 10% below projections last year.

- But our new product line and cost efficiencies should allow us to meet or exceed expectations this year.

4. Chronological. This pattern takes your listeners through a temporal sequence that elaborates your message.

Say your message is, "We have met our project commitments on schedule."
Your bullet points might sound like this:

- When we launched this project, we said we would complete the installation in three years.
- In the first year we achieved the goal we set.
- In the second year we were ahead of schedule.
- Today all of our commitments have been met.

To decide which structure to use, pause after your message, and choose your pattern. And if you have time to think in advance, all the better. Eventually the decision will become second nature. Having a message and bullet points will guide you through your impromptu remarks. Fill in the words as you speak.

Provide Structural Signposts

Do everything you can to help your audience follow you. If you have three reasons, flag them with "The first reason," "The second reason," and "The third reason." Or just "First," "Second," and "Third." If your structure is "ways" do the same. If you are using situation/response, begin the discussion of the situation with, "So our challenge is" or "We have a great opportunity." And begin your response section with, "So how can we best respond?" If you're using the chronological pattern of organization, flag each time frame as you enter that part of your structure. It might be "In the past," "Today," and "In the future." Or it could be "When I first joined this company," "Not long after that," and "Today."

Why the need for this structural scaffolding? Quite simply because your audience can't see your text—there are no PowerPoint visuals that show "Point 1, Point 2, Point 3." So you have to show them with your signposts. Listeners will thank you because they'll stay on the journey with you as you move through your structure.

The Power of Structure: Two Examples

Let's look at how structure works in a script—with two examples.

This first script shows a leader at a consulting firm speaking to a team about a client pitch. His structure shows the ways the pitch needs to be prepared.

GRABBER. We have a great opportunity on Monday, presenting to this client.

MESSAGE. I know we can make this a winning pitch.

STRUCTURE: WAYS. There are several ways we can do that.

- First, we need to present a clear, compelling description of the program we'll deliver.

- Second, we need to specify how we'll help them reach their target audience.

- Third, we'll have to show the tactics we'll use to get their users excited about it.

CALL TO ACTION. So let's all do our homework, go into the presentation well prepared, and leave no doubt we can deliver the results they want.

This second script uses the situation/response model. It's a real-life example that was delivered by Ian Gordon, a senior vice president at a grocery chain, to a group of employees.

GRABBER. Thanks for coming today … it's great to have you here. I'd like to begin with a story from earlier in my career, when I headed up the detergent business at Unilever.

MESSAGE. I found that only by talking to front-line employees could I solve the problems we had in packaging our products.

STRUCTURE: SITUATION/RESPONSE.

- The assembly lines that handled our packaging operated much slower than they should have. Executives at head office were puzzled and disturbed by this persistent problem.

- My conversations with employees in the plant provided an excellent solution: reduce the number of package sizes from 14 to 4. We implemented those suggestions and productivity soared.

CALL TO ACTION. This story illustrates why you need to stay close to your team, listen to their ideas, and give them the support they need to do their jobs better.

All inspiring leaders speak with a clear structure. And they do so not only to be motivational but also to get their views across in tough, contentious situations. Jamie Dimon, chairman and CEO of JPMorgan Chase, speaks with such clarity. In the following example he uses "reasons" to take issue with a reporter who snuck into an employee-only conference call and wrote an article on how JPMorgan Chase was going to use government money to buy weakened competitors.

- "First, I don't think it's right to sneak onto an internal phone call like that.

- Second, we hadn't even received the [government] money yet.

- Third, the person he quoted wasn't even in a position to know what we were going to do with the money.

- And fourth, that employee even said something that essentially contradicted [the reporter's] point."[2]

Leader-like speaking is clear, direct, and compelling.

Learn the four patterns for developing your message, use them, and flag them. If you do all this, your impromptu comments will be persuasive. Part IV of this book will provide many more examples of how these four patterns can work for you.

13 Beginnings and Endings

The Leader's Script begins and ends with the audience. Start by engaging your listeners with a grabber so they'll want to listen to what you have to say and conclude with a call to action that asks them to act on what you have said. In between, you'll want to deliver a message that has the power to persuade them. If you are successful in all this, each conversation will be an act of leadership.

Open with a Grabber

"You had me at hello," from the movie *Jerry Maguire*, sums up the engagement you want from your audience at the outset. Whether you're speaking to a roomful of colleagues, your boss, or a group of friends, draw them in with your first words. If you speak without reaching out to them and engaging them, it's likely nobody will listen to you. That's particularly true for impromptu speaking, because in the helter-skelter environment of today's world—where you're competing for people's attention with smartphones, emails, and interruptions of all kinds—it's impossible to "hold the room" or even hold the attention of one person, unless you acknowledge them.

The grabber can bridge to your audience in various ways. You can call them by name, mention something about them, refer to a point

they've brought up or a conversation you've had with them, ask them about themselves, or bring up something of interest to them. The point of the grabber is to create rapport. Your grabber will not only vary with the individuals you are speaking to, but it will vary according to the impromptu situation at hand. Here are some situations and appropriate grabbers for them.

If you encounter a colleague in the hall, your grabber might be: "You're the very person I want to see," or "I just heard something that will interest you," or "I want to run an idea by you, do you have a minute?" Beware of grabbers that derail you. For example, if you begin, "Ahmed, how's your family?" he may launch into a long tale about his ailing mother. Or if you say to an executive, "I loved your town hall," she may go on to talk at length about her town hall remarks. Make sure your grabber not only engages your audience, but also bridges to your message.

If you are in a one-on-one meeting, and want to respond to a point someone has made, bridge to that. For example, "Mary Lou, I understand where you're coming from." Or "I agree with your logic," or simply, "That's true." Don't say, "Good point," because you're not there to judge the other person. Your grabber shows you've listened and take the other person's idea seriously. Each time it's your turn in an exchange, begin with a grabber that connects what you're about to say to what you've just heard.

If you're in a group meeting, bridge to the conversation underway: "I believe we have two possibilities: choosing among the existing candidates or broadening our search." If you want to bring a faltering discussion back on track, start with words that suggest consensus: "All of us have agreed that . . . ." or "Time is short and we need a decision." It's all about reaching out to your audience, and finding common ground.

If you're approaching someone who's busy, request (rather than assume you have) their ear. If your boss is at her desk staring at her computer screen, your grabber might be, "Do you have a second?" Or, "Is this a good time to ask you something?" If you phone someone, ask if that person is able to talk.

If you're following up on a previous discussion, your grabber can allude to that. For example, you might explain to your boss, "You asked me to interview the candidate for the VP position, and I've met with her." In a coaching session with an executive, I might open with: "When we first met, you said you'd like to work on your presence. Let's begin." These opening lines will get the attention of your listeners.

When you want to take issue with what's been said, show sensitivity. Don't begin with "I disagree" or "On the contrary" or (worse still) "You're wrong," or that tired cliché, "With all due respect." Instead, start with something more collegial: "I understand where you're coming from. Let me share my perspective." Or you might simply say, "Yes, and I see it somewhat differently." Always reach out to your audience in a positive and constructive way. Doing so shows that you've been listening, and others will be more apt to listen to you.

A grabber is also important in high-stakes situations like job interviews. Bridge to the person interviewing you by thanking her for the meeting. Go one step further and say why you are impressed with her company. Over the years I have interviewed many people for positions in The Humphrey Group. I always took notice of whether the candidate opened with comments about our company. I was more excited about interviewing someone who was excited about us.

Think of your grabber as a verbal handshake. It builds a connection with your audience and makes your listeners want to follow you. Once you've done that, you can get on with your message—you'll have their attention and can lead.

End with a Call to Action

The Leader's Script ends where it began—with your audience. The call to action typically asks your listeners to act upon your message. It can also suggest what action you will take on their behalf, or it may outline collaborative action that you'll take together. Once this follow-through action takes place, you will have led.

The call to action can take myriad forms.

First, it can be a handoff to someone you're talking to. So in a conversation you might say, "That's my view, what are your thoughts?" Or "Can you make that happen?" If you are in a group setting, prompt the group by saying, "Let's do some brainstorming." Your call to action invites the other party to continue the conversation.

Second, your call to action may request a decision. Let's suppose you're with your boss and you've made a strong case for proceeding with a project. Your call to action might be: "So, I'd like your approval to move forward with this program," or (still stronger) "So I take this as a 'yes' that you agree we should proceed with this project."

Third, your call to action can specify concrete steps that are needed to begin a project or launch an event. If you're planning a leadership retreat, for example, you might conclude: "So I'd like our team to organize our next leadership retreat. Lynn, please coordinate the panels; Abi and Shawn, I'd like you to work on the logistics; and Niamh, I'll leave it with you to choose a keynote speaker." These "marching orders," when delivered with a collegial and respectful tone, can inspire your team to get the job done.

Fourth, your call to action can be a statement of encouragement. You might say to an individual on your team, "I see that you are excited about this job opportunity in the HR department, and I encourage you to pursue it." A call to action for someone who has missed out on a job opportunity might be, "There will be other opportunities that come your way. Keep an eye out for them."

Fifth, your call to action may convey an ultimatum. A client told me: "There was one particular investment that I recommended, and I presented it a couple of times. Questions were raised, and we had to address those questions. And so the third time I raised it, I said, 'I'm hoping this is the last time I'll be talking about this company. We need to close on this investment. I want to know if it's a yes or a no.' We got closure on it."

Sixth, your call to action may inspire collaboration. You may ask for teamwork, for sharing of goals, for a partnership of some kind. You might conclude: "Let's both work toward solving this problem by being more transparent with each other." Or if you're a manager you might say to a project lead, "Keep me in the loop and I'll support you with any resources you need."

Your call to action, like your opening grabber, should engage your audience. But the call to action plays an additional role: It gives legs to your message by transforming an idea into actionable steps. In so doing, it makes your script an act of motivational leadership. Indeed, the Leader's Script, described in these past four chapters, has the power to turn every impromptu conversation into a motivational moment—as you engage, enlighten, and inspire action in your audience.

Part IV
Impromptu Scripts for Every Occasion

14 Meetings

F ew activities in the business world are as all-consuming as meetings. Studies show that "busy professionals" attend more than sixty meetings every month[1] and spend approximately 40 percent of their time in meetings.[2] CEOs spend a full 85 percent of their time in meetings of various sorts, including scheduled and unscheduled meetings, brief encounters, conference calls, and networking events.[3] Put another way, top executives spend only 15 percent of their time alone not speaking with anyone.

You as a leader have a wonderful opportunity to influence and inspire in these meetings. Listen attentively, build upon the ideas of others, and when you speak, take time to collect your thoughts—even amid the cross fire that often takes place in meetings. You will not only be bringing better thinking, better decisions, and better attention "to the table," but you will be creating a profile of yourself as a leader day in and day out.

The examples in this chapter will show you how to craft your impromptu remarks for common meeting scenarios. The remaining chapters in Part IV of this book discuss how to create scripts for job interviews, networking events, elevator chats, toasts and tributes, informal speeches, and Q&As. In all these settings, the not-so-hidden secret of success is preparation.

Let's look at four common types of impromptu speaking in meetings.

Project Updates

This one you should knock out of the park. You know it's coming so get ready. Your boss asks for an update on a project or a string of projects. Realize that project updates are always a little more than just that. What you're really doing is selling your boss, and anyone else in the room, on your work and why you think it matters—and why it should matter to them, too.

To do that well, you need to avoid the mind-numbing, fact-based approach: "This happened, that happened, here's where we are, blah, blah, blah." It's a poor idea to provide that jumbled-up selection of good news and bad news. I learned the dangers of that tack in my first corporate job. I presented good and bad news about my projects, and wondered why my boss glared at me. I soon realized my job was to sell the projects and show they were in good hands.

Your remarks need to sound spontaneous—but you'll want to have a few notes as memory joggers. The end product should be a thoughtful status report. So jot down notes in advance about how you'll position each project. Start by writing down a positive message for each project, no matter what stage it's in. Then write down or type out several reasons or ways your project can be shown to be in good shape. On your way to work, run through that messaging in your head. You don't need to memorize it word for word (in fact, *don't*), but you do need a mental outline that will guide you through your project update.

When it's your time to present, begin with your grabber. If you're presenting to your boss, you might say, "You'll be pleased about Project X." Then set forth the positive message: "It's on track to deliver higher revenue for our salespeople." *Always* make sure your message inspires. If your group is underperforming, don't hide the fact, but have a message that commits to turning the situation around. Poor results? Show why they'll get better.

Once you've delivered the above message, move to your proof points:

- First, this project will help us identify new markets.
- Second, it will allow us to tap into those markets.
- Third, it will provide metrics to measure our success.

Finally, your call to action ("Stay tuned!").

Such a script will allow your boss to sleep well. Position every project in this way, and you'll demonstrate your leadership and build confidence in your team. Just don't sound boastful or self-aggrandizing. When you've got successes to your name you can be humble.

Briefings

Briefings are much like project updates, but they usually focus on providing an overview of a current situation—a new business opportunity, a recent initiative, or an up-to-date view of the economic environment. Again, you know this one is coming—and you can prepare. Don't bring into the meeting more than a few notes—*if any*—but store the outline in your mind. Things can go wrong if your script is not well organized.

I once worked with a vice president whose first draft of a briefing to a senior executive committee lacked coherence. It was an info dump that said nothing, and was beyond boring. It sounded like this:

Good morning. I'm here to provide an economic update for you.

You've recently read in the media about many issues that challenge our bottom line. However, when we review that data, it is largely—although not entirely—positive. The economic recovery is continuing.

What are some of the problems? The European political scene. Housing markets are weakening. Consumer debt is a concern. . . .

I asked him to stop delivering—we both could see that his audience would have been confused about what he was arguing. We worked together using the Leader's Script to anchor his thinking with a strong message. Here's the revision:

> GRABBER. Good morning. I know you, as our senior management team, are keenly interested in our business environment. I'm pleased to provide you with an economic update.
>
> MESSAGE. It's a positive one: The pace of recovery is accelerating, and that's good news for us in the insurance business.
>
> SITUATION. The signs of recovery are abundant.
> - Positive GDP growth
> - Improving retail sales
> - Strong corporate data—high profit margins and cash positions
>
> RESPONSE. Our investment returns have benefited from these developments.
> - Equity returns are strong.
> - Bond portfolios beat expectations.
> - Credit quality is higher.
>
> CALL TO ACTION. As we work on our next quarter projections, we should see evidence of this favorable economic news.

What a difference! The Leader's Script spells salvation to anyone who wants to brief people in meetings. The outline can be jotted down in advance, and mastered mentally. Or if you feel more comfortable taking the notes with you, sketch in the outline on a small note card or the back of a business card, and bring that to your meeting. The preparation will serve you well in the moment of delivery. In fact, this VP got "kudos" from his executive committee—and they will remember him as a clear-thinking leader.

Sharing Ideas

In meetings, you are expected to share your ideas. Let's say you've been working on an HR project for the past four months. Or you've just finished reviewing the spreadsheets on costs and expenses. You might not be scheduled for a project report or briefing at the meeting, but you should be prepared to speak about your ideas. You want to make a good showing when questions are directed at you. And even when no one has a specific request, you can often enrich the dialogue by sharing your insights.

It pays in all these cases to know what you want to argue, and how you'll back up your ideas. Let's suppose you're the finance guy, and someone turns to you and says, "Tell us about this new investment we just made in the oil service industry." Without preparation, you might only come up with the name of the company, what it does, and the fact that you spoke to its management, etc. etc. But such facts do not suggest your expertise or insights. Far preferable would be the following script, which shows a strong, clear point of view.

> GRABBER. Glad you asked, Bill.
>
> MESSAGE. We have made a major investment in a company called Terracor, which we believe has great value.
>
> STRUCTURE.
>
> (SITUATION): Terracor is an exploration and development company with tremendous resources that will serve it well for years to come. Right now, we believe, the market is underpricing its reserves. By looking at similar transactions, we believe its reserves should be valued at a dollar a barrel. But the market is only pricing them at 25 cents a barrel. That's a huge difference.

(Response): So we saw Terracor as a bargain and made a $100 million investment. We view it as a good, long-term play. But we'll also win big if they're acquired by any of the major oil companies.

Call to Action. We'll closely watch developments and keep you up to date.

The speaker has an excellent command of his subject matter, and comes across as a savvy, clear-minded individual who presents a compelling argument. Who in the room would not feel the portfolio is in good hands with this individual making the decisions? He has used the Leader's Script to great advantage.

And while the name and details of the company have been changed, this is a real example of a young man I worked with who went on to establish an investment company that's a top performer in its category. His name is Jonathan Bloomberg and he is CEO of BloombergSen. Communicating well is thinking well, and performing well.

Collaborating

So much meeting time is spent in repartee that you'll want to be proficient at working with others to build collaborative solutions.

There is no better example of how collaboration can work in meetings than one provided by Rich Bellis, my editor at *Fast Company.* He explained to me: "One of the first things I noticed after joining *Fast Company* was that my coworkers were comfortable disagreeing with each other without things getting heated or personal. When a writer or editor brings up a news event or a question of interest, it usually isn't a finely honed story angle yet. After others weigh in, you can usually tell whether or not there's enough there to run with. But whichever way it goes, there's rarely any sugarcoating or snark in the dialogue."

"In fact," says Bellis, "It's all about the idea. Recently a couple of other editors, a staff writer, and I were batting around potential

headlines for a story we're running. The first couple I proposed got shot down right away—the writer suggested a key phrase that might be more interesting. Then another editor said, well, actually, this *other* idea in the story might be the better thing to focus on. I disagreed, pointing out that the first concept was more likely to interest readers. Finally, we wheeled back around to a totally different headline than the first few we'd considered. Because everyone was focused on the same straightforward goal—finding the right headline for the story—there was simply no time to get possessive about any one idea, and subsequently no chance for the discussion to turn personal."

This is an excellent example of leading in the moment. No egos. No defensiveness. No politics, just collaboration for the sake of finding the best idea. In such repartee, someone—or everyone!—may challenge you or ask a pointed question about something you've said. Don't react or fight back. For example, if a colleague says that a deadline for your project does not seem feasible, listen to their reasoning. Maybe they're right—as in the *Fast Company* example, it's good to be open to other opinions besides your own. You can learn a lot by listening.

But if you believe your deadline is viable, use the Leader's Script template to build support for your thinking. Begin with a friendly grabber ("I'm glad you asked about that. I know that deadline may seem tight.") Next, pause and think out your message and deliver it ("But I assure you we will meet our deadline.") Pause again, and bring together in your mind your proof points. Then deliver them ("#1 Our team's on schedule. #2 Our technology is up and running. #3 Our trials have been successful.") Close with a call to action ("So everything's on track with that timing").

You'll make life easier for yourself if you can "game out" some of the repartee you might encounter at the meeting. Creating a few responses in advance will enable you to come across as thoughtful (and intelligent!) in the heat of vigorous exchanges.

Everyday meetings are a crucial venue for leaders in any organization. They provide you with an opportunity to reaffirm basic values and move forward the projects that you're committed to. But to achieve that success, strengthen your skills in the ways suggested in this chapter. Mastering those techniques will help you lead in the many meetings you attend each day.

15 Job Interviews, Networking, and Elevator Conversations

During my years in The Humphrey Group, one of my most rewarding experiences has been helping young people prepare for career interviews. This began when a client asked me to coach his daughter for her medical school interviews. Thanks to the work we did together, she aced the med school interview, was accepted by the medical school of her choice, and eventually won a fellowship in emergency medicine. She is now a highly respected emergency MD at one of Toronto's leading hospitals.

Few impromptu speaking situations are more important than those in which you need to "sell" yourself. These scenarios, discussed in this chapter, include job interviews, networking events, and elevator conversations. In each case it pays to develop a well-targeted script and answers to potential questions. Doing so can make all the difference in your life and your career. Just ask the young MD in the opening story. She is crazy about being a doctor and her entire career was shaped by that ten-minute interview for which she diligently prepared and rehearsed.

Job Interviews

With professional jobs at a premium, you'll want to prepare a winning script for every interview. Jay Rosenzweig, founding partner of Rosenzweig & Company, a global executive search firm, suggests how to start: "Get hold of a job profile for the position you're applying for and meticulously map out your qualifications in relation to the skills and experience required."

Once you've done that, create a script that shows why you're a good fit. You'll be well served if you write out your script in sentence form, rather than putting down brief jottings. That way you'll be able to internalize the flow of ideas.

Begin with a grabber that thanks the interviewer for the meeting. Show you know something about the interviewer and are excited about the company. Then write down your key message (some version of "I believe there's a good fit between what you're looking for and what I can bring"). Next, sketch in your proof points. Let's say you're applying for a position in a design firm. Your points might be the following:

- My education equips me for this role.
- I am a seasoned designer, with a portfolio that reflects the skills you are looking for.
- I've also been a business builder—which is an area you mention in the job description.
- My values will enable me to be a strong leader in your culture.

Each of these points may be discussed in detail at the interview—so make sure you have texture in the form of sub-bullets for each of these four. It's helpful to have career stories for each point.

End by asking about next steps. ("I've enjoyed our meeting—and I look forward to the prospect of working in your firm. What are the next steps?")

Now internalize your script. You won't necessarily deliver this material in the same order or in the same language as what you wrote down. After all, you don't want to be the candidate who walks into the interview and, unprompted, launches into a script. You'd be coming on too strong and appear presumptuous. The best approach is to let the interviewer lead the conversation and draw upon your script to answer her questions. For example, she might say, "Tell me why you are interested in this position," and you'd tap into your grabber and key message ("I'm excited about this company, and I feel I'd be a good fit for the role"). Then explain. During the interview, continue to draw from your script—as questions come your way, or as you want to make a point. The career stories you've inserted into your script can be used to answer questions. Keeping your script in mind, you'll sound (and be!) confident and cover your points. And you won't leave thinking, "Darn, I wish I'd mentioned that other thing."

To be well-prepared you'll also want to write down the questions you might be asked and answers to them. See the chapter on Q&A for techniques.

How important is this prep work? It's everything. As Jay Rosenzweig explains, "I sometimes meet with candidates who I know are highly qualified, but for whatever reason, they don't have the communication skills to sell themselves." It's this prep work that transforms a strong background into a strong pitch—and a job offer.

Networking Events

Important self-promotion also goes on at networking events. Develop your lines and you'll be able to seize opportunities at these gatherings.

Group events. When preparing for a group event, first figure out why you're going and what you want to get out of it. And no, "Some new contacts" isn't a good answer. What do you want those relationships to lead to? Find out who will be there and decide if

there's anybody whose title or company catches your eye. If so, they're your target. Study their profiles on LinkedIn and other social media. An executive I know says, "When I'm going to an event I'll message people on LinkedIn who I think might be at the event, and I'll say, 'there's a conversation I'd love to have with you. Let's connect there.'"

Write down the messages you want to deliver to those key people. Get those short scripts framed in your mind. If you've identified some-one you'd like to approach, figure out what you're going to say. Maybe you want to ask an executive for some career advice. Approach that individual and wait until there's a pause in the conversation. Then go for it. Begin with your message: "I'd really love your take on where I should go next in my career."

Then move to your bullet points:

- You know the PR field really well.
- I'd be happy to tell you more about my goals.
- I'm at the point where I need expert input like yours.

End with your call to action: Suggest that the two of you grab a coffee to chat about your next move.

Just make sure you show sensitivity when making your approach. I consider myself a confident networker—yet over the years I've learned some key lessons. I once was at an invitation-only Catalyst event, and as I entered the room I saw a CEO I knew speaking with a group of colleagues and admirers. I was glad to see him there. I approached him and the five or six people around him, and shouted out, "Hi Jim." I thought since we knew each other he would suspend his conversation for me. But that was naïve. I didn't have his attention and felt foolish that I had spoken. So put on your diplomatic hat when you enter a networking situation. Target the people you want to talk to, but wait until they are alone or open to your conversation.

Being prepared for these networking opportunities will give you confidence and purpose. As one VP said to me, "I find that small talk can be very draining unless I have an agenda. When I'm not prepared I feel that I can't wait for the conversation to be over. But by game-planning the situation, it's much, much easier."

One-on-one networking. Networking also takes place on a much smaller scale when you're meeting with a single person for career or mentoring advice. Again, there's a need to be focused and to know what you want from the encounter. That will help you prepare your script.

Take advice from the best. Executive Ian Gordon told me, "I don't do a lot of networking, but people network with me. I always ask them, 'What do you want from this conversation? Do you want career advice? Do you want contacts on my Rolodex? Do you want to bounce an idea off me? What exactly is it that you want?' A lot of people don't tell me what they want. They just show up. I try to project what I think they want and tell them what I can."

Gordon continued: "There is one guy who does it really well. He came into my office, we opened the conversation with some childhood memories, and he got right into it. He was asking for connections in the industry, because he was in a job search. I have a lot of connections and he followed up with all the senior level people I introduced him to. At his request, I approached a CEO who agreed to interview him, and who in fact gave him several more connections. It was a really good session. He got what he wanted in half an hour."

Recently, I worked with a young graduate, Nick Palombo, who demonstrated just how focused one has to be to make use of a one-on-one networking situation. Nick was the son of a client and explained to me that he was interested in UN Peacekeeping—his area of focus in graduate school. So I helped arrange a meeting between Nick and the Canadian ambassador to the United Nations, Marc-André Blanchard. Ambassador Blanchard could see the young man's passion and introduced him to Chief Superintendent Barbara Fleury, director general of International Policing, RCMP.

Nick had done his homework about Canada's role at the UN (and knew his own qualifications well), so he was prepared for this spur-of-the-moment meeting. As he told me, "I had already looked Ms. Fleury up on the Internet and found a lot of information about her and I thought if I were to get hired by somebody at the mission, it ideally would be her." Nick spoke so enthusiastically and openly about his career aspirations that Ms. Fleury said, "So you're here because you want my job!" Undaunted, he replied, "Yes, I would love to be sitting where you're sitting, and one reason I'm here is to learn what steps to take to realize that dream." She gave good career advice to Nick, and left the door open for future discussions. The secret to this successful encounter was that Nick knew what he wanted, he was well prepared, and he seized the opportunity to share his career goals.

Elevator Conversations

A third way of promoting yourself, your department, or your company is the "elevator pitch." This term refers to a variety of interactions—only some of which actually occur in an elevator. It is a metaphor for short, on-the-fly pitches you might make anywhere, often to a senior person. It's an appropriate metaphor because elevator pitches—like the rides—are brief. As well, they involve quick encounters with key individuals—executives, team members, clients, your boss, your boss's boss. Having an "elevator script" in your back pocket will maximize your chances of success. But most elevator pitches can't be entirely developed in advance. So keep key leadership messages in mind and create short scripts around them when the occasion calls for it.

Promote yourself. Elevator pitches provide excellent opportunities to advance your own reputation or "brand." Let's say you're in an elevator and your CEO steps in. It's just the two of you. Collect your thoughts then introduce yourself. Tell her that you've just joined the company and are proud to be working on the firm's new social media strategy, and give two or three reasons why you feel that way.

The elevator doors then open, and you have made a critical contact. If you've presented well, your messages will be remembered, as will you.

The same self-promotional strategy can be used at a meeting, reception, or in the coffee room. I have a client who often gets her coffee in the morning at the same time her CEO does. She could simply say, "Good morning" or "Did you find the traffic heavy?" Instead, she sometimes shares what she's doing for the company, which investments she has brought in, and how well things are going. Some people might think such self-promotion is intrusive—and it can be, so pick your moments—but what CEO would not want to hear about the good work his people are doing? These encounters have proven valuable for her career.

As a seasoned HR executive said to me, "When you're looking to grow your career—you have to know the one message you want people to remember about you. It might be that you are looking for a job, fulfilled in your present role, or positioning yourself for another kind of opportunity. It really boils down to this: What do you want them to think about you when they walk away?"

"Is it always the same message?" I asked the HR executive.

"Your pitch changes with time and with each networking opportunity," she said. "For example, I might know someone as an HR leader, but if they're interested in becoming a board member, they have to rewrite their elevator pitch and sell themselves as a potential board member."

A well-thought-out pitch is important for any new situation you encounter, and the best ones have the elements of the Leader's Script. Here's a good example, delivered by a woman who is introducing herself at a seminar (the names have been changed):

"Hello, I'm Estelle Vaillancourt. I am a vice president of HR at Bank ABC here in New York. My role is to create a positive working environment for our employees. I've been with the bank for four years,

and have enjoyed my work immensely." That short script, with only a grabber, message, and call to action, is sufficient for brief encounters. If you want to go longer, or are prompted to do so, add some bullets (your structure). Ms. Vaillancourt might elaborate: "I have three areas of responsibility: (1) ensuring we have a supportive culture; (2) developing a strong career path for employees; and (3) making our bank top tier in employee benefits." Everyone should have such an elevator script "in the ready." But remember to scale yours to the situation.

Promote your team (or your group). Elevator pitches can also showcase your team and the projects they're working on. Only indirectly are these career pitches—although, of course, boosting your team will help your prospects for advancement. One of my clients, a chief financial officer at a big tech company, told me he prepares for impromptu elevator chats by developing mental notes for each executive he might find himself with. He does this because one day he'd been with his CEO in the elevator and forgot to share an exciting program his group had been working on. Each "pitch" in his mind is designed to advance his team's agenda. So, for example, if he sees the company's president walking down the hall, he'll stop him and ask, "Would you be able to speak to my team when we have our 'All Hands' meeting next month? We've achieved total buy-in on the new strategy, and they'd love to hear from you."

These elevator conversations can enhance your career, because in promoting your department or group they leave an impression that you're a go-getter who's always thinking and collaborating even on the fly. Let's say a young manager is in the elevator with a VIP who just spoke to a roomful of women. The manager was inspired by the talk and says to the VIP, "I was at the women's event today. I loved your story. I'd like to make an appointment with you to follow-up on one of the issues you raised." The elevator doors open and, seizing the moment, she says to the VIP, "If it's OK, I'll send you a meeting invite." Assuming a "yes,"

she'll get to know that VIP and get her guidance on a project her team is undertaking.

These chance elevator encounters are excellent opportunities to gain the respect of VIPs. But conversations like these don't happen entirely in the moment. The young manager had already thought of that idea before she saw the VIP. And when the opportunity came, she went for it! That's the power of a prepared mind and script.

If you're prepared, every elevator chat with one of these targeted people can be an opportunity to discuss programs your team is working on. You might tell a colleague in sales, "I'd like to get your feedback on this idea I've been turning over about picking up some new customers." But don't stop there. Develop the idea by stepping out of the elevator and continuing the conversation if your colleague seems keen.

Promote your company and its products. A third type of elevator pitch is the one promoting your company and its products.

People will often say, "Give me your elevator pitch for that product." They mean, "You have thirty seconds—persuade me why we should invest in or buy what you're selling." That conversation usually doesn't take place in an elevator. But in fact, there's a contest called "The Elevator World Tour," which was launched in Toronto's CN Tower. Entrepreneurs were invited to come to the Tower—which has one of the tallest elevators in the world—and pitch their businesses to investors as they rode up to the top floor. Today the contest takes place in elevators all over the world. Contestants are paired with judges who ride up the elevators and listen to the pitches. Investors give the lucky winners seed money for their firms.[1]

Happily most of us don't have to scale the heights while pitching our product or company to would-be clients, investors, or partners. But we all must be good at it if we want our business to thrive. And there's an art to it.

Murray Wigmore, then head of the Japanese division of a Pharma company, told me, "One thing we instituted at the company—and I was a firm believer in it—was the elevator pitch. It was based on the idea that every one of us has a product or something that we are selling. I trained the sales force in how to do this. Good executives will make sure that whomever they're talking to will walk away with exactly the message they want them to walk away with. They should ask, 'What do I want them to remember about this conversation?' Or 'Why should people do business with us?' In sales the elevator conversation might be the answer to: 'What problem can you help us solve?'"

Wigmore told me a story about an encounter he and his colleagues had a few years ago. "We had our executive meeting in Toronto. Afterward, we went to an outdoor patio, and began chatting with the group at the table next to us—a group that included a director of marketing. We thought we'd have some fun, so we asked if we could practice our elevator pitches in front of them, and we invited the director of marketing to choose the best elevator pitch. There was no contest. The director pointed to the person who had practiced her elevator pitch the most and said, 'I would definitely buy from her.' She knew nothing about our company, but the elevator pitch made all the difference."

"What distinguished the winning pitch?" I asked. Wigmore replied: "It was (1) simple; (2) jargon-free; and (3) focused on the value we would bring."

Elevator conversations allow you to make the most of brief encounters. Handled right, they will enhance your career prospects, highlight the accomplishments of your team, and promote your company and its products.

Self-promotion is the currency of getting ahead in any organization. It helps shine a light on your aspirations and skills. Preparing strong, impromptu scripts will help you thrive in these three crucial situations: job interviews, networking events, and elevator conversations.

16 "Just the Big Picture"

A management consultant I know was invited to speak to a hundred executives at a mining conference. This was a dream assignment because it held the promise of new business. The consultant prepared a thirty-minute presentation and was introduced with high praise. Just as he was about to begin the keynote, he was interrupted. It was baseball season and the executives in the room wanted to watch the end of the final game of the World Series. They told the keynoter he could begin as soon as the game ended—it was the ninth inning.

But alas, when the game was over, there were only ten minutes left for the presentation. The consultant went to the podium, stared at his script, and struggled to pick out the passages that would carry the message on his slides. His narrative was filled with "um's," "ah's," "I'll skip over this," and "I'm not sure I have time to elaborate on this point." He grew flustered and incoherent. The audience was disappointed and embarrassed for him, and the company refused to pay his fee.

How many times has each of us faced a similar situation? A meeting convenor or executive has told us time is tight, saying, "Just give us the big picture." These words can be scary.

· There's no better case for relying on the practices discussed in this book than when you're asked, at the last minute, to turn a long presentation into a short one. This was an ability displayed by Gorgias of Leontini, a fifth-century BC Greek orator. He "prided himself on his ability to adapt the length of his speech to any circumstances and claimed to be able to speak with extreme brevity or at the greatest length on any subject."[1] According to Plato, though, it was much easier for Gorgias to go long than short! It's tough to compress.

Here's a brief guide to shrinking your presentation on the spot.

We're Out of Time—What *Not* to Do

Let's say you've been allotted thirty minutes for your presentation. Then, as you're about to begin you're asked, "Can you scale it back to five minutes?" Or you've prepared a five-minute progress report with slides, and you're told to wrap it up in two minutes.

The worst thing you can do is skim through your entire presentation or report, frantically trying to figure out what to say and what to delete. This approach is often characterized by talking too fast and occasionally discarding a slide with the comment, "That's not important," or "We'll pass over that one." Your audience will either feel they're getting short shrift, or conversely, wonder why you included unimportant slides in the first place. And the executives won't forget that you couldn't adjust to their expectations.

Create Your Micro Presentation on the Spot

A far better approach is to bring your impromptu skills into play and create a shorter presentation on the spot. There are three ways to do this.

First Way: Scrap the Slides and Deliver Your Thinking

This approach involves presenting your key ideas—*sans* slides. If you used the Leader's Script in preparing your presentation it will have all the key elements of a good impromptu script—grabber, message, proof points, and call to action. If your time is reduced tell your audience that you will give them the key messages of your presentation.

Adeola Adebayo, a principal at OMERS, takes this approach when she's asked to scale back her presentation. She'll say to her audience, "In the few minutes I have, I will share my thinking with you. The details are in the presentation, which I'll make available to you. And I'll be happy to speak to any of you offline." Then, following that opening (GRABBER), she structures her abbreviated remarks by explaining: "This is what I want us to invest in. This is why I think it's a good investment. And here is how I think we should do it." Her approach goes back to the Leader's Script: This is what I believe (MESSAGE), this is why I believe it (STRUCTURE), and this is how we should act (CALL TO ACTION). That's a brilliant formula for any micro presentation.

Preparation is key to improvising. As Adebayo explains, "You basically have to know your stuff, inside and out. Before the meeting you need to be prepared for the thirty-minute presentation. And within that you need to know what the highlights are—what your key points are." In fact, bring a set of cue cards that have the key messages on them—just in case you're asked for the micro version. On one card put your message, on a second your first main point, on a third your second main point, and so forth, ending with a card for your call to action. On those cards include a few stats for each point. That way, you've got your mini-presentation right on those cards.

There can be great advantages to recasting a presentation *sans* slides. As one of my clients tells his team, "The messaging is more important than the slides. So scrap the slides and tell me what you believe and

why I should believe it too." You're paid to deliver thinking, and this is exactly what your audience will get with this approach.

Second Way: Select Key Slides

A second way to downsize your presentation is to focus on the few slides that present the key elements of your talk. In preparing your presentation, create an outline that has all the components of the Leader's Script—grabber, message, proof points, and call to action. Do this even before you create your visuals. Then design the visuals around this template. If you're asked to speak in less time, use only those slides.

Here's how. Put up Slide 1 [the title slide] and deliver your grabber. You might say, "You have asked for a presentation on this initiative because it represents a major investment for us." Next, put up Slide 2, which should contain your message. Say, "This presentation makes one strong point, and it's this. . . ." Next present your proof points. You might show one slide for each point—or if you've only got five minutes, show a summary slide of all three points (make sure your presentation has such a slide). Finally, conclude with your call to action slide—tell them what you're asking for.

Be sure to save this mini-presentation of four to six slides as a separate file, next to the complete version. Then it will be ready to use if needed, and will save you from clicking past all the other slides you don't have time to address.

Third Way: Just Your Message

There may be occasions when you don't even have time to deliver a version of your presentation's structure. Your boss may rush by and say, "I've got to run. Give me the gist of your presentation." Or you may find yourself in a situation where someone needs the simplest version

of your talk. This was the case for Murray Wigmore, when he was in a former role at Hewlett-Packard.

He had just given a presentation at McGill University in Montreal on "Life Beyond the Laboratory." In the talk he described in vivid detail what it was like to bring applied science into the business world, as he had done in his own career. After the speech he was approached by a professor who said, "I have a very talented student who is thinking of going on in science, but he's entrepreneurial and needs to hear your message. If you have a minute could you talk to him about why he could benefit from getting an MBA instead of pursuing a Ph.D. in science?"

Wigmore told me, "at that point I had to take the content of the 25-minute speech, and bring home the message in a few minutes to a young person who was going to build his life on what I said. It was one of the most inspiring impromptu pitches I ever gave."

There are times when you, too, will have to distill your presentation for one person. Often this comes in a hallway conversation, an elevator chat, or a client meeting. So always carry in your mind the one message you want to get across.

Be prepared to shrink your presentation in any one of the three ways described in this chapter. If you can do that, you'll be able to sell your ideas to anyone, in whatever time they have.

17 Toasts and Tributes

An executive I know wanted to pay tribute to a retiring staff member at a luncheon. He asked his team for anecdotes about this individual—and then built his impromptu remarks around those stories. At the end of the meal, he stood up and began his speech: "Chris is a memorable figure. One colleague will remember him for being late, another for his crazy sense of humor, and still another for his antics as a party animal." Each point was fleshed out by the speaker in embarrassing detail, and he concluded by saying, "So we'll always remember you, Chris, for the things you may wish to forget!"

Everyone laughed—Chris the loudest—but no one was laughing inside. They were embarrassed for Chris, for the executive, and for those who had provided the comments.

Even though you want to be entertaining when you offer a toast or tribute, never let humor supersede leadership. Always adhere to the following guidelines that will help you delight your audiences.

Creating Winning Toasts and Tributes

The formula for a successful impromptu tribute or toast is simple: be positive, do your research, and use the Leader's Script.

Be positive. When thinking out your toast or tribute, stay positive. There's nothing wrong with humor—usually. It can make for a memorable wedding toast, but take care that your humor is not cutting. The executive in the opening example erred badly in collecting and using embarrassing stories about the honoree. If the speaker had instead asked for "a few inspiring stories about Chris," he would have been more inspiring himself. Or—even better—if he had taken the time to think how he felt about Chris, and jotted down an upbeat message and a few supporting points from his own reflections, he would have sounded more sincere. Comments that are even mildly insulting, when delivered in front of a large audience, will be long remembered. So look to your heart for true and positive sentiments about the individual you're honoring, and stay on the "high ground" while speaking.

Do your research. No matter how good a speaker you are, there is a need to gather the best material. Knowledge of the person or group you're praising always counts more than impressive but empty words of flattery. No one will be impressed by generic, off-the-shelf comments. A wedding toast that announces, "Maria is a wonderful person. We all like her," will draw yawns and lead to the surmise that you really don't know the bride. If you don't have enough information yourself, ask friends or colleagues. Remember that your mandate is to celebrate, not to roast that person.

The need to research your remarks is important even when you know a lot about the person you are honoring, because you have to sift through the knowledge you have and find the salient truths about that individual. I remember preparing my remarks upon my dad's death, and jotting down notes about how my dad loved to ride his motorcycle, drive his beloved Porsche, sail his boat, and serve on the National Ski Patrol, all well into his nineties. These were the things I focused on when I said my dad lived life to the fullest.

Use the Leader's Script. This template will serve you well—even in these brief remarks. Otherwise our minds can wander and we will find ourselves chattering away in front of a live audience, or worse still, blowing it by saying something embarrassing. You don't want to pay tribute to a bride by saying, "We're all so glad she found Ronnie, because the guys she was dating before him were real losers."

Collect your thoughts *before* speaking to avoid such blunders. If you're the best man at a wedding, you'll ideally have time to develop your notes. If you're at a lunch and hear that in five minutes you're going to give the tribute, ask yourself, "What's my message about this person or event?" Once you have that, jot down a few supporting points. And even if you decide on the spur of the moment to "say a few words," don't jump into high gear until you have your message. Otherwise your remarks might be a train wreck, as in this chapter's opening example.

Not all the elements of the script will be present in every toast or tribute—occasionally remarks can be as short as a single sentence. (That sentence will be your message. For example, "Let's toast to Louis—a great mentor to us all.") Still, even in a brief tribute you should manage to incorporate most or all the components of the Leader's Script. Here's how to prepare a brief gemlike tribute.

Begin with your grabber. This statement draws the people in the room together and introduces them to your subject. For example, you might say, "It's a pleasure to have this celebration to honor Aditi's contribution to our company." Or "Good evening. I know we're all delighted to be here for Brett and Stephanie's wedding." Or "It's a pleasure to offer a tribute to my beloved niece, the bride." Now you have a captive audience!

Next, move to your message. The message is the most important sentence in your remarks. It will shape and unify what you say, and it should be credible, inspiring, and uplifting. If you're celebrating

the groom, you may want to say: "Alex has all the qualities one dreams of in a best friend." Don't say, "Alex is the best friend I've ever had"—otherwise you might offend others in the audience who thought they were your best friend.

If you're paying tribute to an individual, consider some of the following approaches to crafting your message.

- Choose a quality or attribute that distinguishes that person. It might be "values," "loyalty," "dedication," or "exquisite taste." For example, "Andrew is a person whose deep sense of character has been an inspiration to us all." Or "Dimitri has a taste for the finer things in life" (culminating in his choice of his lovely bride).

- Focus on the impact that person has had: "I am delighted to offer a toast to our president, Gregory Munch, who has enriched the lives of so many students in this university over the past twenty years."

- Build the message around the history of a relationship: "I toast to the decade-long partnership between our two companies by offering the ten top reasons I'm so proud of it."

- Explain what that person means to you (as a mentor, employee, sibling, or friend). "If there's one person I owe my career to, it's Louisa, who has been an inspiring and dedicated mentor."

If you're paying tribute to the members of a team, focus on their achievements, their willingness to collaborate, or their dedication—choose one and make everything else a subset.

Whatever your message, make it compelling, because the rest of your toast or tribute will use that statement as its anchor. And make sure you have only one main message. You've all heard remarks that begin, "There are so many things I could say about Dan, but I've narrowed it down to three." This kind of speech is a grocery list. The audience is left to wonder, which quality is the most important? Were there others? It doesn't hang together.

Provide proof points to support your message. The first example below uses the "chronological" model and the second uses the "reasons" model.

Example 1: Proof Points for a Tribute

Let's suppose you choose the following message: "Harvey is a quintessential entrepreneur." Your proof points might look like this:

- As a child he didn't just have a lemonade stand. He had several that he franchised.

- He went to business school and developed a business right there.

- He founded and grew the firm he's being celebrated for tonight.

- I understand he's got a few more ideas he's about to "hatch."

Example 2: Proof Points for a Toast

Let's say you are offering a brief toast during a holiday party. You would have only three or four proof points, and they would not necessarily be developed beyond a single sentence each. Suppose your message is, "Happy Holidays! We have so much to celebrate!" Here's what your proof points would look like.

- This year has been a remarkably successful year for Techco Enterprises.

- Thanks to the hard work of everyone in this room, we've become the industry leader.

- We've welcomed eight new colleagues who have become key members of our team.

- And we're well set to make next year an even better year.

Close with a call to action. In the first example above your call to action could be: "Let's toast to a true and dedicated entrepreneur." In the second example you may simply ask the audience to join you in

raising a glass and toasting to the celebrated occasion. A call to action may be more explicit. For example, you may suggest that "Salma [who is retiring] will be greatly missed by all of us, but we wish her well as she pursues her dream of becoming an amateur pilot."

Choose the right moment to deliver your remarks. A toast or tribute is best presented when people have finished a meal or are at a crucial moment in an evening; for example, just before the meal is served. Don't speak until you have the full attention of the room. Silence the chatter and draw all eyes to you by tapping your water glass with a knife, clearing your throat, or standing up.

Remember to keep your remarks short and sweet. There's wisdom in the old vaudevillian advice, "Leave them wanting more." Of course, you can be too brief, but the greater danger is wearing out your welcome.

Robert Kennedy's Tribute to Martin Luther King, Jr.

Some of the greatest impromptu tributes of all times give heightened expression to the genre. There is no more profoundly eloquent a tribute than Robert F. Kennedy's eulogy for Martin Luther King, Jr., on the occasion of King's assassination. Kennedy arrived at the Indianapolis, Indiana, airport on April 4, 1968, and heard the shocking news that King had been killed that day. Kennedy had a crowd waiting for him at a downtown rally—they thought they'd hear a campaign speech, because Kennedy was running for president. But Kennedy had only one thought in mind: to honor Martin Luther King. He was handed speaking notes by an aide, but according to a biographer, "he stuffed them into his pocket, preferring to extemporize...."[1] He proceeded to deliver one of the most brilliant impromptu tributes the world has ever known.

Standing on a flatbed truck that held a makeshift podium, he delivered an address that lasted less than five minutes, but moved the world.

His grabber startled the predominantly black crowd: "I have bad news for you, for all of our fellow citizens, and people who love peace all over the world, and that is that Martin Luther King was shot and killed tonight. Martin Luther King dedicated his life to love and to justice for his fellow human beings, and he died because of that effort."

Kennedy spoke about the dangers of acting out of bitterness and hatred. Then he came to his inspiring message, which used repetition to underscore its importance: "What we need in the United States is not division; what we need in the United States is not hatred; what we need in the United States is not violence or lawlessness, but love and wisdom, and compassion toward one another, and a feeling of justice towards those who still suffer within our country, whether they be white or they be black."

He quoted the Greek poet Aeschylus about wisdom coming out of pain. And he closed with an uplifting call to action: "Let us dedicate ourselves to what the Greeks wrote so many years ago: to tame the savageness of man and to make gentle the life of this world. Let us dedicate ourselves to that, and say a prayer for our country and for our people."[2]

This brilliant impromptu tribute had an immediate impact. Despite rioting elsewhere in the United States, Indianapolis remained calm. And a quotation from this celebrated speech would later be carved on the wall of the Robert Kennedy memorial in Arlington National Cemetery.

Few of us will have an opportunity to craft such long-lived and inspiring remarks as Robert Kennedy offered for Martin Luther King. But we should keep that same passion in mind, and do our best to create toasts and tributes that resonate with the same inspiration that Kennedy showed—inspiration that derived from a heightened sensibility of the person being honored. My call to action to you is to follow the guidelines in this chapter. Be positive. Do your research. Use the Leader's Script. And your tributes will uplift and inspire your listeners.

18 The Impromptu Speech

A vice president I once worked with was asked to introduce a minister of labor at a business luncheon. The executive had prepared an adulatory introduction, but the minister showed up early and needed to speak well before her designated time. When the VP arrived, his introductory remarks were no longer needed.

After the minister finished her keynote address, the master of ceremonies called upon the VP to "say a few words" about the speaker. The executive knew he had to craft an impromptu speech, do so quickly, and make it right for the occasion. The theme of his remarks came to him as he walked up to the podium to address the seven hundred people in the room. He began, "Madame Minister, I am not surprised you were ahead of schedule today. After all, as your speech indicates, you have been moving rapidly to address labor issues in this province." The VP then enumerated a few of the labor issues that the minister had been tackling and resolving. After doing so he concluded, "Thank you for coming today and for staying ahead of schedule on your commitments to this province."

This brief address comprised the perfect impromptu speech—well organized and fully suited to the occasion. The ability to think on the spot, and the guidance provided by the Leader's Script proved a winning combination for him.

One Compelling Idea

The best impromptu speeches reverberate with a single, captivating idea. In this respect, they are like other kinds of impromptu remarks that rise or fall on the key message. You may only have a few moments to pull together your thoughts, as this VP did, but always ask yourself, "What's the key idea I want to leave my audience with?" The executive's central idea (praising the minister for "moving rapidly to address labor issues in the province") flowed out of the grabber ("I am not surprised you were ahead of schedule") and led to the call to action in the final line of the speech. Once you have that message, you're well on your way to a great speech. All you need to do is figure out your proof points, and your call to action.

For example, suppose you're eating dinner at a business function and the MC announces, "We'll be hearing soon from Kahlil, who will accept his award." If you're Kahlil you may be trembling because you didn't realize they expected you to speak. But don't despair: Jot down a single message and three or four bullet points that develop that message. They will serve you well and you'll be glad you were able to pull together a speech that inspired your listeners.

If you know in advance you'll be expected to "say a few words," by all means do your research, create your bullet points, embed them in your mind, and be ready to inspire.

A Perfect Example—Lou Gehrig's Farewell to Baseball

There is no better impromptu speech to serve as a model for you than Lou Gehrig's "Farewell to Baseball." This speech is one of the most moving speeches in sports history, delivered at Yankee Stadium on July 4, 1939. At the age of thirty-six, he spoke to a crowd of 61,000 fans, announcing his farewell to baseball—because he was suffering from ALS, or amyotrophic lateral sclerosis. At first he shook his head "no," indicating that he didn't want to speak. But when the crowd yelled "We

want Lou!" he came forward and delivered the following remarks.[1] The speech has one compelling idea that's delivered throughout the speech.

> Fans, for the past two weeks you have been reading about the bad break I got. Yet today I consider myself the luckiest man on the face of this earth.
>
> I have been in ballparks for seventeen years and have never received anything but kindness and encouragement from you fans.
>
> Look at these grand men. Which of you wouldn't consider it the highlight of his career just to associate with them for even one day? Sure, I'm lucky.
>
> Who wouldn't consider it an honor to have known Jacob Ruppert? Also, the builder of baseball's greatest empire, Ed Barrow? To have spent six years with that wonderful little fellow, Miller Huggins? Then to have spent the next nine years with that outstanding leader, that smart student of psychology, the best manager in baseball today, Joe McCarthy? Sure I'm lucky.
>
> When the New York Giants, a team you would give your right arm to beat, and vice versa, sends you a gift—that's something.
>
> When everybody down to the groundskeepers and those boys in white coats remember you with trophies—that's something.
>
> When you have a wonderful mother-in-law who takes sides with you in squabbles with her own daughter—that's something.
>
> When you have a father and a mother who work all their lives so you can have an education and build your body—it's a blessing.
>
> When you have a wife who has been a tower of strength and shown more courage than you dreamed existed—that's the finest I know.
>
> So I close in saying that I might have been given a bad break, but I've got an awful lot to live for.[2]

Creating a Successful Impromptu Speech

If you want to hit a "home run" with your impromptu speeches, follow Gehrig's example. Whether you are receiving an award, retiring from your company, being honored with a surprise party, or celebrating your

birthday or anniversary, this speech is an excellent template on which to build yours. Here's how.

Collect your thoughts. Gehrig, according to his wife, wrote some remarks but hadn't rehearsed or brought a text with him.[3] In doing this, he avoided the perils of either reading a speech (too formal) or winging it (too casual). If you know in advance you'll be expected to "say a few words," by all means do your research, create your speaking notes, embed them in your mind, and be ready to inspire. Whether you have days or minutes to collect your thoughts, be sure to have notes in your mind.

Open with a short, personal grabber. Gehrig's opening made reference to the people at the stadium and your first words should invite your audience into the speech. Gehrig's calling them "fans" endowed them with a special relationship to him. And acknowledging that they knew he was ill also builds an empathetic bond. Begin your speech with a similar reference to those in the audience. For example, "Friends, your being here means the world to me," or "Colleagues, you've found a way to surprise me as never before," or "Hi everybody. Wow, what a sight. You make me so proud."

Choose an inspiring message. Gehrig has a simple but poignant message: "Today I consider myself the luckiest man on the face of this earth." At a moment when everyone in the stadium was in tears—and Gehrig himself was crying—he offered a message that broke the spell of that awful news and uplifted his audience.

When you create your message, state how you feel, as Gehrig does, in an inspiring way. Here are some examples:

- "I feel like the luckiest/most fortunate/most privileged/happiest person in the world."

- From a CEO: "I am thrilled that we have turned the company around and can look forward to new markets, new customers, and a new vision of success."

- From an award winner surrounded by family, mentors, and colleagues: "I feel humbled by this honor because you are the very people who have made my career a success."

- From a philanthropist: "I believe this occasion shows the power of giving back to society."

Provide your proof points. Show your audience why you believe in your message. Gehrig brilliantly develops his argument by having a series of short, sharply focused points showing the many people that have made him feel so lucky in life. You, too, can build a speech around the individuals or groups who are in the room. Imagine you are being honored in retirement—each of your points might refer to individuals who have been important in your career. Or if you're being honored at a birthday party, have points that call out several people who have come to the party and have played a special role in your life. You can also build your points around groups: your partner, your family, your friends, your colleagues, your mentors.

Follow Gehrig's lead by using some of his language patterns. One of the most compelling aspects of his proof points is the repetition in his language. It accentuates the parallel ideas. He begins many statements with "when," as in "When everybody down to the groundskeepers," "When you have a wonderful mother-in-law," "When you have a mother and father," "When you have a wife." He creates a cadence that builds powerfully and advances his message. As well, ending many of his points with, "Sure, I'm lucky," further reinforces his main message.

Take a page out of Gehrig's book, and use repetition to tie your points together and reinforce you message. For example, you might say in a retirement speech: "I'll always remember how my family has supported me." And for your second point, "I'll always remember how my colleagues have inspired me." And for your third, "And I'll always remember how my team has fulfilled my greatest expectations." This repetition gives rhythm and cadence to your remarks.

Close with a call to action. This last component of your impromptu talk suggests future action, which can be physical or emotional. Gehrig's conclusion is: "So I close in saying that I might have been given a bad break, but I've got an awful lot to live for." He envisions a life that will continue, even though he knew he only had a few years to live.

Your call to action can take many forms—it can be future action taken by you (as with Gehrig), by the audience, or by you and the audience. If you are being honored with an award for business excellence, your call to action might look ahead to the goals you have for your firm. Or if you're being honored at a birthday party, you might look ahead with the thought, "Given the great friends and family who surround me today, I look forward to many more birthdays and cherished moments like this one. Isn't that, after all, what life is about?"

This address by Lou Gehrig, which adheres to the Leader's Script, is a wonderful example of a short, simple, but heartfelt impromptu speech. It was given at "Lou Gehrig Appreciation Day," and is an excellent model for all those times when you are speaking to friends, family, colleagues, and others—whether the occasion is a birthday, wedding, anniversary, retirement, or completion of a successful project.

19 Q&A

H ippias of Elis, a prominent Athenian orator of the fifth century BC, was the master of Q&A. He would appear before large crowds and respond to any question put to him. He told Socrates he had never been confronted with a question he couldn't answer. While few of us have Hippias's supreme confidence, the best impromptu speakers are well informed and adept at answering questions. You'll discover in this chapter how to respond to questions by preparing thoroughly, structuring your answers, and avoiding the traps that can ensnare speakers.[1]

Getting Ready

What you do *before* answering questions is as important as what you do *while* answering them. Preparation involves mastering your content, listening carefully, and pausing before speaking.

Master your content. A solid grounding in topics that pertain to your company, your field of expertise, your team, your clients, and your competitors is the foundation for handling Q&A well. It helps, too, to have a general knowledge of other fields you can draw from. Mark Zuckerberg in 2015 resolved to read a book every two weeks on "different cultures, beliefs, histories, and technologies."[2] And an article in *Fortune* quotes one of his colleagues as saying Zuckerberg's desk typically has a pile of books on it, and "for a while there was a book on free-space optical communications," a technology Facebook

was interested in.[3] Leaders need that rich storehouse of information to master their subject and respond to questions intelligently.

When preparing for Q&A, organize your material around questions that might come up. Phil Mesman, a portfolio manager at asset management firm Picton Mahoney, told me, "When I deal with clients, I try to anticipate what they might ask. Then I group those questions into categories. So for example, if there are certain things happening in the market—if corporate bonds are going higher or lower—I know people will ask about that. By focusing material around questions, I can have an opinion on each group of questions, and move the conversation toward what I want to say." If your Q&A is a high-stakes situation—like a job or media interview—take the extra time to create a bullet-point outline for each response to a question you are likely to be asked.

Listen fully to the question. Once the questioning begins, be sure to listen carefully so you can respond to just what was being asked. Ernest Hemingway once said: "When people talk, listen completely. Most people never listen."

Pay attention to the *entire* question—many people tune out while the question is being asked because they're trying to formulate their answer. But jump-starting your answer can cause you to answer only part of the question or misinterpret it. You might be answering the question you *think* is being asked, but if you had listened fully you'd hear the questioner say at the end, "So what I'm really asking is. . . ." You'll miss that. So don't start to think of your response until you've heard the full question.

Also listen for the question *within* the question. Sometimes the actual question is not the real question. For example, if you are a manager and a team member asks you, "Will there be layoffs with this merger?" the real question may be, "Will our group be affected?" Or "Will I lose my job?" You'll want to answer the underlying question too. You might say, "I can't speculate about overall layoffs, but I can

tell you that our PR department is not likely to be affected because the other firm doesn't have a PR group."

Pause before speaking. That pause is also part of your preparation. It allows you to collect your thoughts, and begin to structure an intelligent reply. Often people rush their responses. Rob Borg-Olivier, a vice president in The Humphrey Group, observes, "When people fail to answer well it's usually because everything comes out at once. Nine times out of ten people race to answer a question without pausing. They just go, go, and go, and sometimes within 30 seconds they recover, but often they don't achieve the clear thinking they'd like."

During that pause begin to map out your response. If you have mentally outlined this answer as part of your preparation, you're home free. But if not, you'll need to create your answer on the spot. In pausing before speaking you will be able to design your script, or some elements of it, and sound more intelligent than as though you blurted out whatever came to mind. That moment of silence might feel uncomfortable, but it will show that you're confident enough to reflect seriously on what's been asked. The pause signals that your answer will be a thoughtful one.

Developing Your Answer

Your answer needs to make a point clearly, and that doesn't always happen. Brad Katsuyama, portrayed as the brilliant hero in Michael Lewis's *Flash Boys*, was interviewed by Matt Levine of Bloomberg News. Levine asked him this probing question: "What's your advice for the next you—someone who works on Wall Street, has a big idea, and wants to change the world?" Katsuyama's response goes into a broad range of topics without answering the question:

> It was a very hard decision to leave RBC [The Royal Bank of Canada], because there's a certain level of comfort working at a large firm and being part of the system. I do think we're shifting to a

more transparent society. What that does is cast a brighter light on how people make money. We don't have any issue with people making money. That's just capitalism. We're capitalists at heart, we're a for-profit entity. But I think how people make money is going to be a greater focus. If people are thinking about doing something different with their lives, just think about the incentives that are there for you to do what you do. And if you don't believe in that incentive structure, finding a different thing to do with your life isn't as risky now as it was in the past. I think the world is more receptive to people trying to do things differently.[4]

While Katsuyama's response offers interesting points, it is difficult for the listener to connect the dots and come up with a simple, unified message. Indeed, sometimes the brightest and most knowledgeable people will answer with narratives that are full of expansive thinking, but don't pass the "what's he saying?" test. And that's where a template for structuring your answers comes in.

The Leader's Script will enable you to structure your response so you provide pointed answers. Its four components—grabber, message, proof points, and call to action—will together help you craft strong, clear, focused answers.

Here's the drill.

Begin with a grabber. This bridges from the question to your key message in several possible ways:

- It shows agreement or empathy with the questioner ("We understand your concern and take it very seriously.")

- It plays off against the question ("I can't comment on that, but I can tell you that. . . .")

- It neutralizes negatives (If an interviewer asks, "What's the biggest mistake you ever made?" you might respond, "I regret that I didn't get into this profession earlier.")

- It answers questions of fact. If you are asked a yes/no or factual question, your grabber can answer it head on. For example, if you're asked, "Did your company make a major acquisition last year?" your grabber might be, "Yes, we did." If you're asked, "What were your employee engagement scores last year?" you might say "9 out of 10."

Your message comes next. Leaders who wish to motivate their audience need to speak on a higher plane. Your strategy is to move from the grabber to a high-ground message. Let's say you're asked whether any new product announcements are anticipated. Your grabber might be a simple, "Yes, at the end of this month." And then comes your higher-ground message: "You'll find that our new software will be a game changer in the field of voice recognition." Or if asked whether your firm's three new wells have begun producing, your grabber might be, "Yes, they have," followed by your message, "And they are exceeding our expectations."

Structure with proof points. In some instances the grabber and message may be sufficient. For example, in answering a question about whether your background will allow you to do the job you're applying for, you might simply say, "Absolutely. I believe my entire career has pointed to a position like this." But if you haven't yet elaborated your background to the interviewer, this is your chance to do so. Back up your argument with a set of clearly structured points about your background.

The proof points can be organized in a variety of ways (as discussed in Chapter 12). They can be "reasons," "ways," "situation/response" or "chronological." For example, if you're applying for medical school, and you are asked "What attracts you to medicine?" your message might be, "The opportunity to help others." Then provide the reasons you believe that: (1) You've worked at a refugee health center and found it

gratifying; (2) You have a grandparent you're nursing through COPD; and (3) You are inspired by your mom's medical practice.

Close with a call to action. This defines next steps. If you're a politician, you might say, "I believe voters will see us as the party that can restore economic prosperity." A business leader might ask her team to "keep up the great work." And a CEO might conclude with "I am excited about our company's future and the growth we envision." The key is to build on your message and define a future that your audience can believe in and be part of.

Two Examples

Let's take a look at two well-structured answers.

The first is a CEO's response to a question from a financial analyst. The analyst asks this head of an integrated oil and gas company: "How much would your firm be willing to spend for a drilling site in the North Sea?" The reply:

> (GRABBER): We have no specific number in mind. (MESSAGE): But we are always on the lookout for growth opportunities, and if such an opportunity comes up we would evaluate it carefully against our global criteria. (Point 1): It would have to be financially attractive. (Point 2): It would need to be the right size. (Point 3): It would have to fit our overall strategy. (CALL TO ACTION): We are always open to expanding our presence on the world stage.

What makes this a superb answer?

- The speaker doesn't speculate.
- The answer sets forth a high-ground message about the company as a clear-thinking organization.
- The proof points (ways) make every acquisition sound strategic.
- The call to action projects a continuing pattern of successful growth for the company.

This next example is an answer from an employee to his boss's question. The boss asks his IT specialist, "Are you sure we are spending the right amount on systems?" The reply:

> (GRABBER): Yes. (MESSAGE): We have a carefully monitored plan for IT spending. (Point 1): We buy only what's necessary for the business. (Point 2): We put out bids for competitive pricing. (Point 3): And we make sure that our spending creates value for our company. (CALL TO ACTION): So you can have confidence in our spending decisions.

What makes this a good answer?

- The employee doesn't get defensive.
- He takes the high ground with a compelling message.
- The message is developed with clear, succinct points.
- The call to action encourages the boss to have confidence.

In these two examples the question provides an opportunity for a high-ground leadership message. Questions may be soliciting information, but it's best to respond by bringing forward an answer that inspires.

Avoid the Traps

Q&A isn't always a gentle interaction. Most of the time, you can expect at least a few questioners to be tough on you. Even before you get to your message, recognize and avoid the following traps that trip up less-seasoned speakers.

1. **Don't repeat a negative (even to deny it).** President Richard Nixon infamously stated "I am not a crook," responding to allegations directed at him regarding his involvement in the Watergate scandal. Those words came to haunt him. Don't repeat a

negative in the question. If someone asks, "Is your firm putting all
its eggs in one basket?" avoid replying "No, we are not putting
all our eggs in one basket." Just imagine a media headline, "NO,
WE ARE NOT PUTTING ALL OUR EGGS IN ONE BASKET,
SAYS CEO."

2. **Don't evaluate the question; answer it.** We often hear speakers
   say, "That's a good question." This can be a stalling tactic—an
   effort to buy time while thinking. Or it may be a sincere response
   to a thoughtful question. But whatever the reason, it's rather
   condescending to evaluate questions. Your role is to answer them,
   not judge them. And if you say some are good, are the others bad?
   Just answer them.

3. **Don't speculate.** Even when someone asks you for a number that
   you'd like to give, don't do so if that number is confidential or if
   you aren't sure of it. Instead, say, "We have not released that
   number yet, but I can tell you that. . . ." If you don't know the
   number, say, "I'll be glad to get it for you."

4. **Don't tacitly agree to false statements.** If someone puts forward a
   falsehood or erroneous fact about you or your company, politely
   correct it—or the audience will assume it is accurate. Suppose
   someone says, "Given the fact that your firm has an aggressive and
   competitive culture, how do you explain the large percentage of
   women at senior levels?" Begin by dismissing the erroneous
   statement. Say, "Actually, we have a very inclusive culture." Then
   answer the question, "Our open culture has attracted top female
   talent to our company."

5. **Don't ask the questioner questions.** Once the question has been
   asked, it's your turn to respond. If the questioner has not been
   clear, then it's unlikely she will be any clearer if you give her
   another crack at it. So interpret the question as best you can, and
   answer it without further probing. Simply say, "As I understand it,
   you're asking me. . . ."

6. **Don't be negative.** Sometimes speakers will frame a question with negatives about you, your company, your career, your colleagues, or your competitors ("Are you saying that your company is not yet profitable?"). Don't repeat the negative. Say "We expect to be profitable next year." In the same vein, if your questioner asks you a loaded question laced with inflammatory or prejudicial language, don't go head to head. Reply coolly and move to the high ground—have a message that distances you from the negative or contentious language. For example, imagine the question is, "How can we believe you if your projections for last year were so far off?" Reply: "The fundamentals of our business are extremely strong—our operations are firing on all cylinders, our cost-cutting program is on target, and we are trending ahead of our guidance on production for the year. So we feel confident we will meet our projections."

7. **Don't get frustrated by questions that are "speeches."** After one such question, an executive I know responded, "I'm not sure if that was a question or a statement." Such a response looks bad! Be gracious even under these circumstances. Do your best to carve out something that individual has said amidst the verbiage, and answer that.

8. **Don't answer questions that are patently outrageous.** Occasionally you'll be asked an "off-the-wall" question that can throw you for a loop. For example, a boss might say to an employee, "You're late. Did you have a wild night last night?" Instead of answering, simply smile and move to another topic.

9. **Don't lose your cool.** When Abraham Lincoln's political opponent Stephen A. Douglas falsely accused him of taking a certain position, Lincoln jokingly responded that his opponent's "specious and fantastic arrangement of words," was like proving "a horse chestnut to be a chestnut horse."[5] There's a place for such humorous repartee, not only on the political stage, but on the corporate stage. Just make sure it doesn't offend anyone.

The high ground is where you want to be. If your audience wants simple, factual answers they can turn to their smartphones. Back in 2011, IBM's "Watson" proved the quickness of artificial intelligence by defeating the human champion on the TV quiz show *Jeopardy!* Watson accumulated its wide-ranging knowledge by "reading" the equivalent of millions of books.[6] Apple's Siri can answer an extraordinary number of questions as well. Leaders, however, need to do more than provide informational answers. They must inspire, enlighten, and deliver key messages that lift the thinking of others to a higher plane.

Part V
The Impromptu
Stage

20 Rehearse Your Remarks

When Texas Governor Rick Perry was campaigning in 2011 to be U.S. president, he was asked in a TV debate how he would cut federal spending. He responded, "It's three agencies of government when I get there that are gone: commerce, education, and the uh ... what's the third one, there? Let's see."[1] He made it worse by adding "Oops." One of the other debaters offered a suggestion. But it was too late. Perry will always be remembered as the presidential candidate who blew it by forgetting that third agency. Ironically in 2017 Perry was appointed to head up that very department he had forgotten: energy.

Such stumbles usually come because the individual did not rehearse. That lapse is particularly surprising in a political debate, which has an element of predictability. After all, most candidates have their talking points down cold. Wisdom dictates rehearsals with someone to play the opponent(s). This holds true whether in politics, business, or personal situations.

This chapter focuses on rehearsing, and introduces Part V of the book—getting ready to perform. Rehearsals are a great way to move into high gear, but once on the small stages of extemporaneous speaking you'll also need to choose your words, use improv techniques, and achieve a leadership presence with your voice and body language. All these topics will be covered in the remainder of this book.

But first, the rehearsals. Successful spontaneity is a practiced art. There are times when you'll want to rehearse your remarks out loud because it can make all the difference in client pitches, job interviews, Q&A exchanges, impromptu speeches, difficult conversations, and (even) marriage proposals.

Client Pitches

Pitching clients can be unnerving, so it's best to practice. When I established The Humphrey Group I made many cold calls to CEOs. These were high-stakes calls that could deliver tons of business. So jotting down notes and rehearsing my pitch again and again was a way of life. When the CEO didn't answer, I left a recorded message—explaining who referred me and why I'd like to meet. Promising to call the executive's assistant and set up a meeting would be my call to action. Often I'd push the rerecord button and deliver my pitch again. It was an arduous process—but rehearsing the pitch was key. As a result, I often got the interview and grew my business.

The same prep went into my in-person client meetings. I remember once an executive asked me to speak to his senior team. It was a big opportunity because if the team liked what they heard, the CEO would bring my firm in to coach his full team. After carefully writing out a set of notes the night before, I drove to the event early to rehearse. In my car outside the hotel, I burned the script in my mind by reading it out loud. Not memorizing the script word for word, but internalizing the thinking and logic. The presentation came off like a dream and we got the business.

Those rehearsals made all the difference. Knowing my material well enabled me to be confident and more eloquent than I would have been with a hazier recollection of what I wanted to say. Whether you're an entrepreneur, a salesperson, or a team leader, selling your ideas takes practice, and rehearsing will help you stay on message.

Job Interviews

Rehearse for job interviews, too. Practice until you know your script thoroughly and can successfully field any questions thrown your way. This takes work, but it's worth it.

Sussannah Kelly, executive vice president, DHR International, one of the largest executive search firms in the world, regularly rehearses candidates for CEO positions. She fires questions at them, and gives them feedback on their answers. According to Kelly, "what they learn from these rehearsals is that it's not about them. It's about how they can help the company. Sometimes candidates will come out of a job interview and say, 'I was great,' but they won't get the position because they didn't focus enough on the company."

Rehearsing successfully for job interviews is well-illustrated by a leader I worked with. She was being considered for a CEO position and worried that she'd panic and speak too fast during the interview. She asked for help, and a colleague and I prepared her.

We helped her with her script then bombarded her with questions. For example, "Why do you feel you are suited to this role?" "What kind of a leader are you?" "How do you handle pressure?" We helped her organize each answer around a grabber, message, proof points, and a call to action. Her answers came from material in her script. We also threw some "wild cards" at her—questions that she didn't anticipate, such as "Tell us about a moment when you didn't have an answer to a problem."

Next, we videotaped her. We noticed her body language was weak—her arms were folded and her hands had small, busy gestures. She also spoke too fast—as she had feared—rattling off her points without pausing. We gave her this feedback, and worked with her on several rounds of retakes. She also practiced at home, delivering with stronger body language and a slower pace.

After all this work—a total of four hours with us and six hours at home—her interview finally came, and it went off without a hitch. She is now a CEO.

The vast majority of individuals we rehearse for job interviews are successful. These are students, managers, executives, and others who devote time to practice. If you don't have a coach, ask a friend, colleague, or family member to rehearse you. You'll be glad you did.

Networking Events

If you want key networking encounters to go well, rehearse them. Such was the case with Cynthia Ward, a vice president in The Humphrey Group, when years ago she prepared to meet His Royal Highness Prince Philip. At the time, she worked for Nortel, a global telecommunications firm that supported Prince Philip's charity, The Duke of Edinburgh Awards. She was given a one-page Protocol for Greeting Royalty and was told that under no circumstances should she approach the Prince. But Cynthia wanted to make sure she did meet the Prince and had something to say to him. So she researched the charity, determined how much Nortel donated, and studied the protocol sheet. At the reception, the room was filled with the media and local politicians, so armed with her prep work, she made eye contact with the Prince and when he acknowledged her, she was introduced to him. She curtseyed and the conversation about Nortel's commitment to His Royal Highness was under way.

"The preparation paid off," Ward remembers. "He called his server to pour me a glass of wine and we chatted about our corporate support for his charity. He was gracious and enthusiastic, and we would have talked longer, but he was whisked away."

Q&A Exchanges

Q&A dialogue can take many forms—on-stage conversations, conference calls, media interviews, town halls, employee events, and job interviews. Rehearse for all of these.

More leaders are turning to on-stage conversations and media interviews to promote themselves, their books, their ideas, or their products. In every case, you'll do better if you prepare and rehearse answers to possible questions. I was hosted by client companies and business schools when I was on my last book tour. To prepare, I drew up a set of questions and answers, gave them to the host organizations, and learned the answers beforehand. I never answered any question in the same way, but I knew what they'd ask and roughly what I'd say. It made the events much easier for me yet had the semblance of spontaneity.

Even the Q&A dialogue on late-night talk shows is shaped by prep work. "The guest will typically talk with a 'segment producer' before the taping and sketch out a few stories and jokes," says Scott Bromley of The Chernin Group. "This conversation informs the bullet points that are written on an index card on the host's desk. When a host says, 'So, I was doing some research and I read that ...' Or 'Hey, I wanted to ask you about something ...' that's essentially a euphemism for 'Let's talk about the next question I'm supposed to ask you.'"[2]

Smart business leaders also prepare for Q&A. A financial executive I worked with was a pro at such dialogue, because he rehearsed for his conference calls with analysts. Before each call he'd write down all the questions they could ask him, and create succinct, message-based answers. He worked hard at this prep—creating several pages of Q&As. Then I would grill him on those questions and others. I also threw in a few "left-field" questions like, "I hear there's a management shakeup in the works at your company, is that true?" Or "Do you have any plans for a merger?" As a result of these rehearsals, he was terrific on the conference calls.

When your firm decides to have a series of speakers on stage in a talk-show format, make sure they're actually delivering coordinated messages. I went to an event where the speakers were unscripted on stage lounging in easy chairs. They were relaxed, but their thinking was

not well orchestrated. I left wondering what overall point of view this leadership team had—if any. A rehearsal with honest feedback would have been a huge help.

My advice: Rehearse for Q&A situations, whether you're an executive, a leadership team, a prospective employee preparing for a job interview, or a student prepping for a med school interview. Your "coach" for these rehearsals might be a professional trainer, a colleague, or a family member.

Impromptu Speeches

When you've been asked to "say a few words" at an upcoming event, it's a good idea to rehearse. Speakers who don't practice can blow it.

Such was the case with a singer who introduced a choral group touring Mexico when I was visiting there. He hadn't rehearsed or received any feedback from other members of the group (as I later found out). His comments were all about himself, not about the group or the music they would be performing. And that was embarrassing for all. He concluded his remarks with, "I'll be available at intermission and would love to get to know members of the audience. Do come up and speak to me."

Had he rehearsed, he ideally would have gotten feedback on his remarks. He would have done a much better job.

Even the remarkable actor Denzel Washington stumbled when he hadn't rehearsed his remarks for an award ceremony. He was called up to the stage at the 2016 Golden Globes to receive the Cecil B. DeMille Lifetime Achievement Award. But he had not mastered the few notes he brought up with him. "I lost my speech," he said. And then after asking the audience to sit down, and mentioning his son, Malcolm, who was not there, he continued, "You really do forget everything you're

supposed to do up here. I'm speechless."[3] He struggled to read some notes he had crumpled up in his hands and then he began thanking people.

One doesn't expect a speaker in this situation to read a prepared speech, but we do expect that individual—particularly knowing he'd be receiving this award—to be eloquently "spontaneous." All it takes is rehearsing bullet points and speaking with those notes in mind.

Word of advice: Always practice your impromptu remarks in front of a virtual audience so you can deliver well to a real audience—and save yourself embarrassment.

Difficult Conversations

Another impromptu situation requiring rehearsal is the "difficult conversation."

A senior executive we coached wanted to practice a conversation she would be having with a team member who frequently clashed with his peers. She intended to address his behavior, but was concerned that this direct report was a poor listener.

Our instructor, James Ramsay, took the part of the subordinate. Together they explored ways of reaching this individual. The senior leader left the session with much greater confidence. A few days later she called our instructor and said, "You must be psychic. My encounter with him almost exactly followed the script we used. In the role play, you threw up your hands and said, 'Well, I don't think that's on me. That's these other people's problems.' My employee used those exact words. The preparation kept me from being off guard, and gave me the confidence to bring out my key messages. It all went so well. My staff member promised to work on his interactions with colleagues."

A Marriage Proposal

Leadership opportunities come in all areas of our lives, and in our inter-personal relationships we may have important conversations that need to be rehearsed.

I had one such discussion that transformed my life. I was twenty-six years old and had been dating a fellow academic for about a year. Realizing he was the perfect guy for me, I thought, "Why wait until he comes to that conclusion on his own?" Even worse, "What if he doesn't?"

So taking the situation into my own hands, I prepared notes for a marriage proposal. My grabber was that we'd been dating for a full year and seemed so right for each other. My message was that I believed we should get married. My proof points were that we shared academic careers, we enjoyed each other's company, and I had never met a guy who was so devoted to me. My call to action was that I would like to think he felt the same way, but if he didn't we should each move on. The crowning touch of the call to action was that I'd give him two days to decide.

When I had quietly rehearsed and internalized my proposal, I delivered it one Sunday night after a fun weekend. He was surprised—what guy wouldn't be—but he acknowledged he could understand my feelings and would think about my offer. The following night he came to me and said, "I'm not sure I would have made the decision to get married now, but I don't want to lose you." It was one of the best moments of my life, and we were married three months later. My entire life has been shaped by marriage to this special man, and the gift of love we have shared with each other and with our two children.

I tell you this story (with the generosity of my husband) because it describes one of the most meaningful impromptu moments in my life—and it shows just how important it is to collect your thoughts and rehearse for these conversations. Imagine if I hadn't prepared my

thoughts—I might have blurted out, "Just when are you going to propose to me?" or "Don't you appreciate me?" When our emotions take over and our minds are not in gear, we can make statements that we later regret. So rehearse important conversations you may have at home or with friends, and it's likely your relationships will be stronger and more enduring.

All these situations—and others—will go so much better if you prepare your script and then rehearse it. After all, even the most seasoned comics rehearse their lines. Each day before taping *The Tonight Show*, Jimmy Fallon performs his monologue in front of a small, live audience. If you watch, you can see him editing his text as his audience provides feedback.[4] No wonder he is so "naturally funny" on camera.

21 Choose Your Words

Mark Twain once said, "The difference between the right word and the almost right word is the difference between lightning and the lightning bug."[1] In impromptu speaking we may struggle to find the right word but land instead on the almost right word or even the wrong word—followed by apologizing, self-correcting, or rephrasing. The dilemma is that we're selecting our words on the spot—without time to think, edit, rewrite, or polish as we can in scripted speaking. The words tumble out of our mouths as we focus on the ideas we're trying to formulate.

To strengthen your impromptu language, keep the following four C's in mind: be Clear, Conversational, Confident, and Collaborative.

Be Clear

Abraham Lincoln, an inspiring speaker—greatly valued clarity. He remarked: "When a mere child, I used to get irritated when anybody talked to me in a way I could not understand. I don't think I ever got angry at anything else in my life. But that always disturbed my temper and has ever since."[2] Audiences expect that same clarity from you. Yet it's not always easy to achieve clarity in the moment. Here are some things to keep in mind to achieve it.

Think clearly. Unclear language comes from unclear thinking. Too often words roll off the tongue yet they don't present a clear idea. Take this example: A corporate spokesperson in a Q&A with investors states, "What is interesting is that, as a technology company, we do believe in community involvement and so we believe in education and training programs and building capacity in the communities we are active in." In plain English, what does this mean? Too many generalities. Better to be specific: "We are committed to supporting our communities. This past year we helped ten schools set up 'Girls Who Code' programs."

Prune your prose. Take a mental cutting board and slice off extra words.

- Say "We'll focus on," instead of "What we are going to do is focus on."
- Say "We should consider," instead of "I think we should be considering."
- Say "I suggest," rather than "If possible I'd like to put forward the suggestion."
- Say "To Stephanie's point," rather than "It seems to me that there may be something here to consider, something Stephanie said."

Junk the jargon. Speak plainly!

- Delete phrases like "Transform our educational knowledge set" and replace with the more familiar "learn."
- Delete words like *commoditize, optimize, operationalize, utilize,* or anything that ends in -ize or -ized.
- Delete expressions like "paradigm" or "on my radar screen" that have no clear definition.

See Bart Egnal's book, *Leading Through Language*, for a far-ranging discussion of the perils of jargon and how to avoid them.[3]

Be Conversational

Impromptu language should be conversational—marked by the simplicity we use in everyday conversation. Here's the difference between office talk and home talk. A leader at work might say: "Off the top of my head what I'm going to talk to you about is a little bit of the year in review." A leader at home might say, "Let's look at the past year." Being conversational means you use language in the workplace that you'd use outside of work.

Here's how to get rid of office speak and sound more conversational:

Use short words. Winston Churchill said, "Broadly speaking, short words are best, and the old words, when short, are best of all."[4] So don't use "however" if you can use "but." Don't use "in order to" if you can say "to." Don't say "prioritize" when you can say "choose."

Shorten sentences. Your audience can understand shorter sentences better than longer sentences. That's why we naturally speak in shorter sentences in our daily lives. The following before-and-after example shows how conversational a senior manager sounds when she forgoes long sentences. When asked why leading her new team would build upon her strengths, she replies:

Before: "My strengths are coaching and relationship building, and the team that I have inherited is a very good team, and with my coaching skills in this relationship-building area it will be very successful in this sector."

After: "My strengths are in coaching and relationship-building. I've inherited a team that's awfully good. But it needs to build stronger customer ties. I know that together we'll reach that goal."

The revised passage is easier for the audience to absorb (as it consists of sentences that average eight words, compared to the "before" sentence that has thirty-seven words).

Don't be too casual. Be conversational, but be professional. Avoid "yeah," "yup," "nope," "gotta," "you guys," "stuff," "hey," and "whatever!" Use these words with your friends, but such words can sound too relaxed when you're addressing a boss or colleague.

Be Confident

When speaking off the cuff, project confidence in the following ways.

Speak with conviction. Use phrases like "I believe," "I'm convinced," "I've thought a lot about. . . ." Starbucks CEO Howard Schultz uses such language when he says, "Starbucks' best days, I truly believe, are in front of us. . . . I believe sincerely in the future of our company because I believe in all of you."[5]

Filter out the filler. Avoid words like "um … ah … yeah … well … like … you know … to be honest" or any combination of these. They'll make you sound hesitant and unsure. For example, if someone says, "I think, uh, we should, like, hire that person" you might wonder if the speaker is really keen on that prospective employee.

Shun weak words. Watch out for the following anemic language.

- Mincing modifiers such as "I'd *just* like to say something," or "I'm *a little bit* concerned." Or "it's *only* a thought, but *maybe* we should."

- Tentative verbs like "I *think* we should move forward with this project," or "I'm *guessing,*" or "I'll *try* to," or "I'll *see if I can.*" A manager who says "I *think* we can proceed, and I'll *try* to get the budget" won't inspire confidence.

- Past tense instead of present. Saying, "I *wanted* to bring up the fact that," or "I *thought* we should delay the decision" sounds like you no longer believe what you're saying.

- Expressions of self-doubt. For example, "Okay?" or "Right?" or "You know?" at the end of sentences make you sound unsure.

- Excuses and defensive language. For example, "I only came onto this project two weeks ago," or "It wasn't my fault," or "I've tried my best."

- Clichés. These include empty expressions such as the following: "Business is business," "It is what it is," "What will be will be," "Time will tell," and "The customer says 'jump' and we jump."

Watch wiggle words. The most common wiggle words are *perhaps, probably, possibly, basically, largely, hopefully, sort of,* or *quite*. In providing a hedge these make you sound less than confident. If you say "*hopefully* we will find a solution," your listener may not believe you.

Cut the caveats. Common ones (often appearing at the beginning of a sentence) are: "I could be wrong," "It's just a thought," "It's only a suggestion," "This might sound far-fetched," "Don't get me wrong," "This may be a silly question," "That's only my opinion." Suppose a leader says to a team member, "*This might sound foolish,* but you could make more productive use of your time." The caveat weakens the sentence.

Be Collaborative

Many of the best conversations in any organization are collaborative. As American Express CEO Ken Chenault says, "It's not just about being nice. A good teammate says 'Here's what I'm going to do to help you to improve.' It's about putting the team ahead of individual egos."[6] Here are steps that will help you come across as more collaborative.

Limit the language of "ego." Words that can smack of egotism if overused, such as "I," "me," or "my," should be used sparingly. A managing director of finance said to me: "When we talk about employees

coming up for promotion, the candidate should be confident but not arrogant. Arrogance comes across when someone uses a lot of 'I did this' or 'I want that.' I look for people who say 'we did' or 'our team did.'" Of course you can say, "I am proud that our team showed such dedication." Or if someone asks, "Did you design the campaign?" you can reply, "I had a role in the design, but it was a real group effort and we're excited about the outcome." In short, you don't have to disappear from the spotlight entirely, but don't feel you have to put yourself front and center.

Nix the negatives. Collaborative language builds relationships, and is therefore positive. Avoid "I *can't*" or "I *won't*," as in "*I can't* get the budget for this project," or "*I won't* be able to make the meeting." If you cannot attend a meeting, simply say, "I'd love to participate, but I have other plans." Also, avoid expressions that contain "not," as in "I will *not* be attending" or "I'm *not* available." If you're not available say, "Can you come back in a half hour?" If you don't have an answer, don't say, "I don't know." Say, "I'll find out."

Finally, avoid the word "no," as in phrases like "*no* way!" and "*no* problem." Think of it this way: *no problem* is a double negative, and two negatives don't make a positive. So if someone asks you to complete a task, don't say "no problem." Say, "Yes of course," or "I'd be glad to." Suppose your boss says, "Don't you love our new corporate logo?" (And you don't!), instead of saying "No," or lying, find a positive response: "I like its color" or "It's very edgy."

Focus on common goals. Favor expressions such as "This strategy needs to work for all of us," and "Let's look at how we together can create this program." You might ask your direct reports, "What can I do to assist?" Rally the troops with words like the following: "It's great to have all of you here. Our dialogue over the next few days will help us develop a clear and shared understanding of just who we are and what our goals are." Such language fosters the commitment of all team members.

Encourage diverse viewpoints. Use language that encourages people to speak up and share disparate views. It's important that you come across as considering everyone's opinion so you can collectively come to the right decision. A collaborative leader might say: "I've called this meeting so we can come up with a plan for improving employee engagement. I want input from all of you. No matter what your proposal is, large or small—I want to hear it, and we will respectfully respond." Make sure everyone at the table expresses their views. Call on people if they don't volunteer. They may be waiting for an invitation.

Recognize other people. Whether you're in a one-on-one conversation or a group discussion, show your audience that they mean a lot to you. Take time to open with a warm, effusive "How *are* you?" During the conversation applaud your listeners for their input. Say "I agree with you," or "That's a great point," or "Awesome!" In a meeting bring energy to the exchange by saying, "We've got a lot of excellent perspectives here" or "I'm loving this discussion." Reinforce what others say. ("I like your idea about bringing other teams into the project.") Draw out individuals you know have something to offer. ("What's your view on this, Theo?") This is not just building people up for the sake of it; it shows your genuine conviction about building collaborative solutions.

Language is a powerful tool for engaging and inspiring people. Use it effectively in your spontaneous exchanges. Recognize the importance of the "Four C's." Be Clear, Conversational, Confident, and Collaborative. Internalize these principles so when you are speaking in the moment your language is powerful.

22 Use Improv Techniques

This chapter was contributed by two improvisational actors, Dan Dumsha and Angela Galanopoulos. When I decided to write this book, I knew I wanted to tap the expertise of the masters of improv—those who stand up on the stage and face friendly (and sometimes tough) audiences night after night. With that in mind, I turned to Dan, a longtime instructor in The Humphrey Group with extensive experience in improvisational comedy. In good collaborative fashion, he asked fellow improv actor Angela Galanopoulos to cowrite this chapter with him. The techniques they share will help you learn to be "in the moment" and discover how to create collaborative conversations with fulfilling outcomes.

Why Improv Techniques for Leaders?

We improvise every day of our lives. We spend considerable time with others in on-the-fly interactions, creating as we go. Yet, when it comes to impromptu speaking in business settings, many people panic, worrying that they could say the wrong thing or look silly. Indeed, giving an impromptu toast for a colleague can be a minefield, as can answering a tough question on the spot. And the stakes are high—audiences have long memories for our slips of the tongue—and that can cause still more fear when speaking impromptu on the corporate stage.

The good news is that there are techniques from improvisational theater that can dramatically improve your spontaneous communications. Improvisational theater has been around for decades and has gained popularity in business training. Applied improvisation has been used by organizations like Google, PepsiCo, and McKinsey[1] to harness the potential within teams. Among the business schools offering improv workshops are MIT's Sloan School of Management and The Richard Ivey School of Business in Toronto. These programs teach the ability to listen, respond, cocreate, and build toward shared outcomes.[2] As MIT instructor Lakshmi Balachandra explains: "Improv teaches you how to think on your feet and how to react and adapt very quickly to unexpected events and things you may not have planned for."[3] So the concepts of being "in the moment" and cocreation that underlie improvisation are ones that every business leader should master.

Learning to Be "In the Moment"

A key principle of improv is being "in the moment"—being totally centered on the present situation. It sounds simple, but in this world of pressing schedules, multitasking, and insistent electronic devices it can be challenging. Here are three things you can do to achieve this centeredness.

First, don't be distracted by the past. In impromptu conversations it's all too easy to reflect on past events, or imagined judgments of what we've just said. And all too often these reflections are negative. We think, "The last time I spoke to this group, my proposal was turned down. They've probably written me off because of that." Or we reflect in the midst of an exchange, "This isn't going well." We think about how it was "supposed to go" rather than committing to how it is actually going. Dwelling on the past blocks you from any discoveries in the moment and you miss out on how your audience is reacting to what you're saying and what they need from you. Finally there's the

barrage of more off-topic thoughts like, "Did I put enough money in the meter?" or "Did I lock the door?" Such reflections undermine our ability to receive new information and respond to the present conversation. Learn to put these distracting thoughts out of mind by concentrating on the present.

Second, don't focus on the future. Prepare (as this book urges) for your impromptu remarks, and then be "in the moment." Don't fret about the next event or tasks later in the day. If you're thinking, "This conversation better end in time for my next meeting," or "Will I get to the daycare in time to pick up my kid?" you won't be nearly as sharp as someone focused on the moment.

Similarly, don't worry about outcomes. Negative thoughts about the future may well become a self-fulfilling prophesy. If your mind runs to, "What if this all goes wrong?" or "What will my boss think of me as a result of my request to him?" you'll get that less desirable outcome. A colleague shared a story about someone who was concerned that she came across as too aggressive, so when she was about to present to a committee in a job interview she worried, "Will they think I'm too aggressive? Will they decide against hiring me because they don't like my style?" Those thoughts could derail her because she would not be connecting to her real audience, only her imagined audience. Someone who is "in the moment" is much better positioned to connect with their audience and respond to them. If we are thinking ahead to outcomes, half of our brain is off-site and the other half is limping along. Focusing on the future inhibits your ability to connect with others. So stay in the present.

Third, trust in yourself and "follow the fear." If you want to be in the moment, believe in yourself. Self-doubt and fear can be crippling and can lead to inaction or vague communication. Improvisational theater emphasizes the need to conquer these fears by trusting in yourself, embracing mistakes, and experiencing the thrill of discovery.

Actor and coach Del Close was famously quoted as saying, "Follow the fear."[4] He meant that we should benefit from those fears, draw energy from them, and not avoid them. For example, if you're fearful of speaking up at a meeting, don't give in to the fear. Follow it by putting your hand up, and boldly expressing your ideas. If you're afraid an employee has concerns about your leadership, follow that fear by talking to that employee and drawing her out. If you're afraid that a client has not bought into your proposal, follow that fear by asking the client, "What do you think?" or "Do you have any reservations?" If you are hesitating to offer an idea or solution because you are afraid you may be wrong, realize that your contribution may be the needed step on the way to the best solution possible. Trust in your instincts and turn fear into a powerful force for self-affirmation. Don't let fear take you out of the moment; let it be an enabler for you to lean in, trust in yourself, and believe in your ability to get beyond fear and embrace the moment.

What Happens When You Are in the Moment?

Once you are "in the moment," you will be totally centered and engaged in your impromptu conversations. You will be able to respond completely and appropriately. You will surprise yourself and make discoveries akin to the comedic moment in improvisational theater when you seem smarter, cleverer, or funnier than you could have planned.

For example, when Amazon's Jeff Bezos was well into an interview with Henry Blodget, editor-in-chief and CEO of *Business Insider,* Blodget threw Bezos a zinger: "Let's talk about profit, or, in your case, the complete lack thereof." Quick on the uptake, Bezos turned to his audience and said, "This is Henry's version of being nice to me!"[5] This witty response came because Bezos was totally centered—not thinking about how Blodget should have phrased the question or what the audience would think of an unprofitable Amazon.

When you are "in the moment" you will be more accepting of your own emotions, instead of hiding from them. Your inner voice will say, "I'm okay with being nervous. I'm okay with being uncomfortable." It is no longer a fear, but something to accept and explore. You will be in control of how you *react* to these emotions. They will not be ruling you. You'll be observing them and discovering how they motivate you in your conversation. And if you're not afraid of showing nervousness, it will work in your favor.

Cocreation—Improvising in the Moment

Improv actors excel at cocreating with their onstage partners. Cocreation involves working with others by accepting their ideas and then adding to them. Cocreating is a particularly important skill for members of any organization to develop. Solutions don't come from one person or one team—they are developed across, up, and down organizations. Here are some keys to becoming a successful cocreator.

First, cocreate by listening carefully. You can cocreate only if you listen deeply to what is said. That means focusing on the speaker, not on your own next contribution.

Here's a technique that improv actors use to hone their listening skills. It involves word association. Imagine performers standing in a circle. One speaker tosses out a word and the next person puts forward a word that is inspired by that term. Then a third speaker provides a word inspired by the second speaker's utterance. And so on. Each person makes an association only after receiving the word intended for them, resisting the urge to preplan a response. The learning from this exercise is that participants often hear all the words except the one immediately preceding theirs—that's because they're thinking ahead about what word they will provide. This exercise teaches participants to listen thoroughly and not let up on their listening until the previous speaker has finished speaking. In business discussions, such intense

listening will improve the quality of your interactions. It encourages us to hear everything that was said rather than "jumping the gun" and saying something that is irrelevant to what the previous speaker actually said. That deep listening will go far to create shared solutions, whether you're in an elevator, a corridor, or a meeting room.

Second, cocreate by accepting what others offer. In improv, "offers" are ideas, information, or feelings that contribute to a scene. Sometimes they are the suggestions from fellow actors, at other times they are requests from the audience. Improv offers are conveyed through words, tone, and body language—just as they are in a business setting. You don't have to agree with them, but you do need to show that you have received them. In fact, the term "offer" gives us an appreciation for how we should respond. We should be receptive (rather than combative or competitive) when someone shares a thought with us, because an offer is a gift from another person with whom we're communicating. Thinking of it this way encourages us to respond generously even when we don't agree with what's been said.

If a colleague says something you disagree with, accept the offer by saying, "I hear you," instead of "Absolutely not." Or suppose you are in a meeting, and a speaker puts forward an idea that you think is foolish. Apparently everyone else does, too, because the room is stone silent. Accepting the speaker's "offer" would mean responding with a gracious comment like, "Tell us more," or "Can you explain how you came to that conclusion?" Those responses show you have received what the speaker has said. If you and everyone else stay silent, you would be rejecting the offer. Not only would that insult the speaker, but you'd be taking the conversation nowhere, squelching what could have been a valuable and constructive dialogue, and discouraging future contributions.

Third, cocreate by using "Yes, and" rather than "Yes, but." Cocreation also involves building on what others have said using the "Yes, and" technique. In many business meetings, people are just

sitting there waiting for a chance to sound brilliant. When someone delivers a point, these restless listeners are quick to say, "Yes, but," using their response to show how much smarter they are than the last person. They are in the role of "judge" rather than "collaborator." Cocreation involves building on what others have said using the "Yes, and" technique. "Yes, and" is the linchpin of improvisation. "Yes, and" encourages cocreation because it means that others' ideas are not only acknowledged and accepted, but are built upon and advanced. The outcome is always something that could not have been achieved by a single person.

So, in your impromptu conversations, once someone presents an idea, shares a thought, or responds to something you have said, don't rush to prove them wrong, because doing so will shut down the conversation. Say, "Yes, I agree with that point ... and" or, "For sure, that makes sense, and here's what we can do about it." Or, simply, "Yes, and we can do that for you as we've done for other clients."

Let's say you don't agree with the previous speaker's statement. You can still say "Yes, and." So you might respond, "Yes, and we might look at that challenge from a second perspective." Draw what you feel is of value in the last speaker's point of view and combine it with your insights. You'll now have the first speaker as an ally. And the synthesis of viewpoints will almost always be more valuable than any idea that simply opposes the first plan.

In sum, improvisational theater provides valuable techniques for anyone in business or any other domain. Improv shows the importance of being "in the moment," totally focusing on the exchange at hand. And improv actors can also teach business leaders much about the importance of cocreation and the skills needed to achieve those collaborative results. There is no shortage of opportunity in our daily lives to share the stage with others and embrace the excitement of true and present interaction.

23 Find Your Voice

Your voice is a powerful instrument for impromptu leadership. If you're too rushed, too loud (or soft), or seem out of breath, you will undercut your ability to engage others. This chapter discusses how to achieve a strong, confident voice by learning to breathe, grounding your voice, and achieving the ideal volume, tone, and pace.

Begin by Breathing

Learn the power of deep breathing. Each day we inhale and exhale over twenty-three thousand times.[1] But finding that needed wellspring of breath when you are about to speak extemporaneously is not easy, especially when you feel you're in the hot seat. As the rush of adrenalin flows through your body you may pick up the pace of your breathing and breathe more shallowly—with your respiration coming from the chest or throat rather than from the diaphragm. The result? You'll sound unsure, uncomfortable, and anxious. Breathless.

Reclaim that breath, that energy, that life force as a warm-up for any impromptu encounter. Practice these simple exercises.

First, take deep, even breaths. Breathe in for a few seconds, then breathe out for a few seconds. Concentrate on what you are doing and count to two or three as you inhale and two or three as you exhale. Repeat this pattern until you feel much more relaxed.

Second, do a "body scan" exercise in which you consciously relax each area of your body. Begin with your toes, then your feet, your knees, your thighs, your stomach, heart, lungs, neck, and head. This exercise will calm you and send a signal from your body to your brain that you are calm. It's something you can do while listening to others. If you do this you're less likely to get nervous when you speak up. Your voice won't shake and your hands won't tremble.

Third, relax by thinking of a pleasurable scent. Imagine that a favorite flower, one with a strong scent, is before you. Take in as much of the scent as possible each time you inhale. Indulge in it and appreciate it fully. Now notice how this exercise has deepened the breath in your body. See how relaxed you feel and how ready you are to speak.

What if you don't have time to do these exercises before you speak? You're in a meeting and suddenly a question is thrown at you. Before answering, pause, and take a deep breath. That breath will send a calming message to your brain. You will sound—and be!—more focused in your reply. It takes a steady, reliable supply of breath to speak powerfully. When your breath strikes your vocal cords and makes them vibrate, you create a strong, confident sound.

Ground Your Voice

Grounding your voice will make it deeper, stronger, and more credible. In coaching leaders, I regularly get requests from executives who ask me to work with their direct reports to strengthen their voices. I once coached a vice president, and the first thing her boss said to me was: "Rosanna needs more gravitas. She is often in meetings with clients and needs to convince them to invest in our funds. For that to happen, she has to sound more credible." I listened to her and sure enough, she had a voice that was pitched too high, making her sound younger and more junior than she was. *Gravitas* literally means to be "grounded." People with gravitas are taken more seriously because they speak with weight

and substance. Their voice supports their ideas. Men are more apt to speak with lower voices than women, but even some men can benefit from acquiring a deeper range.

> As an exercise, try delivering a short passage—any passage—in your normal voice. Now try delivering it with a slightly deeper voice. Do you hear the difference? Do you sound more credible, thoughtful, and insightful when you ground your voice?

To build this skill, think of the connection between "gravitas" and "gravity." Imagine your voice tugged down by gravity. Actress Lauren Bacall lowered her voice at the suggestion of movie director Howard Hawks and, over time, according to Bacall, she developed a voice that "gives people the impression that I'm formidable, when I'm really quite vulnerable."[2] Why is gravitas so important in impromptu moments? When we are tense or surprised, or rushing as we speak—as often happens in off-the-cuff moments—our voices rise. So gravitas is a perfect antidote to that tendency.

And stay grounded to the very end of your sentences. Some people lift their voices as they approach the end of the sentence—in a pattern called "upspeak"—as if they're asking a question rather than making a statement. No matter how brilliant your words, if you use that vocal approach, you will undercut everything you say by appearing to question each thought. It sounds like you're saying to your audience and yourself, "OK?" "Is that all right?"

Strive for the Right Volume

Find a voice that's neither too loud nor too soft, but strong and confident. If you speak too softly, people will tune you out. You'll sound tentative and unsure. By the same measure, if you're too loud or aggressive, you'll offend people.

It's important to read each situation, as the volume you should project will vary.

- If you're in a meeting, your goal should be to reach the person farthest away from you. Let your voice carry to the end of the room or boardroom table.

- If you're in the elevator and you're talking to someone right next to you, your goal should be to reach only that person. You don't want to broadcast the conversation.

- If you're speaking on a conference call, your voice represents your entire presence. Your volume should be strong and compelling. I encourage people to stand while speaking on conference calls, so their voice will have more power.

- If you're in a cafeteria line and talking to a colleague, speak over the din of the kitchen noise—or decide to keep to pleasantries until the two of you sit down.

- If you're at a networking event and see a client across the room, don't yell—walk over and have a one-on-one.

- If you're in a meeting with lots of intensely vocal people, adjust your volume upward so you are heard. But if you're with softer voices, turn your volume down.

In short, find a volume that is strong and confident, and that is appropriate for each situation.

Adopt a Warm, Committed Tone

If you want to lead in impromptu situations, adopt a warm, committed tone that inspires confidence. Let your voice be expressive and show you're a person who cares about what you say and about those you're talking to.

Being expressive is not easy for some people. I once worked with a client whose tone was flat and expressionless. So we role-played his voicemail message to find a warmer tone. He recorded the following

message: "Hi, you've reached Anthony Abbot. Please leave your name, number, and time of your call, and I'll get back to you." I told him his words still lacked warmth. He gave it a second try adding, "Have a great day," but his tone was still clipped and detached. I suggested, "Let's try again, and as you speak, think of a specific person who might be calling you. Someone you like." He asked, "How about my girlfriend?" His last take was warmer and more inviting. He had found his emotional center. That center is what we must find not only for family and friends, but also for business colleagues.

Hiding your feelings—and yourself—in impromptu conversations weakens your impact. People expect you to "be real" and if you aren't, your words will sound hollow. Find ways to express your feelings. Warm, cordial sentiments build relationships.

Be careful not to sound aggressive or pushy, though. As Chris Anderson writes in his book, *TED Talks*, studies by Professor Albert Mehrabian show that when it comes to communicating our *emotions*, audiences react to our tone even more than they do to what we actually say.[3] If you state, "I like your idea," but your tone is hostile or even neutral, your audience will read you as negative. And if you just rant at people, they'll like you even less and will not hear your words. Always sound positive and supportive of others by maintaining a warm, receptive tone.

In addition, show commitment to your own ideas by expressing them with passion. Demonstrate excitement about what you're saying. Others will hear that conviction and be more likely to embrace your ideas. Your words to a prospective customer might be:

"We in The Albacore Group have enjoyed this conversation with you. We're confident we can meet your needs. And we'd appreciate an opportunity to work with you."

The words—"enjoyed," "confident," and "appreciate"—are expressive. Emphasize those words. If you think of language as a landscape,

determine which words you want to bring into the foreground and which ones you'll let recede into the background.

Pace Yourself

Your pace should be slower than you think. When we speak extemporaneously there's often a huge rush of ideas, words, thoughts, and emotions. As a result, we frequently spew out words at an accelerated pace—faster than we can think and faster than our audience can absorb them. The example below, in a Q&A interview, shows what can happen when a speaker goes faster than he or she can think:

> INTERVIEWER: You've been leading your organization at a very challenging time. Have you gotten over the problems caused by the product defects last year?
>
> EXECUTIVE: I'm glad you asked because I can tell you, um, that there's been a lot of attention paid to this situation and, well, when all is said and done the result has been forward movement for our company. I don't need to tell you, we put the customer first, and that has meant progress for us, you know, and if I do say so, it hasn't been easy and we don't know where this will take us, but I see it as progress and we do want to be open and forthcoming about it.

This executive's answer is a hodge-podge because the words outpace the executive's thinking. Filler words are added to buy time ("I'm glad you asked," "um," "well," "when all is said and done," "you know," and "if I do say so") and there is repetition for no particular purpose (the executive states twice that there's been progress). The speaker's ideas are scattered (progress, putting the customer first, openness, not certain about the future). There's little clarity because the pace is too fast.

Here's how to get the pace right.

First, pause between sentences. This will allow you to formulate your next idea, and it will also help your listeners absorb what you've

just said. Typically the pause between your sentences should be about two seconds. But if the thought you just delivered is a big idea and warrants more time for your listeners to absorb it, make the gap longer. Or, if you need more time to focus your next idea, take that time by pausing longer. If you're worried that the pauses between your ideas will make your audience see you as a slow thinker, don't worry. The opposite is true. Those speakers who pause between their ideas look and sound more confident and thoughtful. It's as though they're sharing something that's truly coming from their minds.

Second, deliver your ideas at a relaxed tempo. You'll be able to eliminate filler words, repetition, and run-on sentences. And you'll have time to structure your ideas more successfully. Each sentence you speak should have a single, clear idea, and if you speak more slowly you'll be carving out that thought more effectively. So take your time—make the tempo of your speaking the same as the tempo of your thinking.

Third, pause between the elements of the Leader's Script. Those breaks are a sign to listeners that you are moving from grabber, to message, to structure, and finally, to the call to action. Those pauses will also give you time to think out those structural units.

Our voices have extraordinary power. According to one study, when participants conveyed their views vocally, rather than in writing, they were judged "to have greater intellect (to be more rational, thoughtful, and intelligent)." They were also seen as more likeable and desirable. As the study's authors explain, "Without even thinking about it, you naturally flood your listener with cues to your thinking through subtle modulations in volume, tone, pace, and pitch."[4] So our voices clearly speak volumes for us. Take time to develop a voice that has the power to reach, engage, and inspire others.

24 Master Body Language

I once coached a bright young financial executive whose job involved speaking to potential investors. He was tall and attractive with a warm, engaging manner, so I assumed he would come across with executive presence. But at our first coaching session, when I turned the camera on and asked him to pretend he was talking to a prospective client, he displayed body language he'd never want to show a client: he nervously pulled his hair, shifted his weight from foot to foot, and occasionally reached into his pockets and jingled coins. He was a bundle of nerves. When I replayed the video, he was horrified. We worked on conveying a more confident body language, and he became an excellent speaker.

Projecting strong body language is important in all situations, particularly in spontaneous exchanges where there is no podium or PowerPoint slides to hide behind. Done well, body language is a powerful asset for those leading in the moment. It draws listeners to us and encourages them to engage with our ideas. It reinforces the substance and passion of our words. It sends important messages about our openness, our warmth, and our interest in the other person. With practice, we can train ourselves to become physically present in a way that inspires others.

Stand and Sit Tall

The way we sit and stand is remarkably important. In her TED Talk and her book, *Presence,* Amy Cuddy discusses why stance is crucial for speakers. Cuddy explains that humans, like all animals, "make themselves big when they have power chronically and also when they're feeling power in the moment." On the other hand, when we feel powerless, "we do the opposite. We close up, we wrap ourselves up, and make ourselves small."[1]

Our daily interactions demonstrate the truth of those observations. People who feel disengaged at a meeting, or who believe they have little to add often slouch or fold their arms. Those who want to make a point will sit up tall and open their arms to gesture. Here's how to develop a stance that projects power and leadership:

- Stand or sit tall—be as tall as you can be.

- Hold your head high, with chin tucked in.

- Keep your shoulders square: don't hunch or slouch.

- Keep your arms open and loose at your side, available for gestures.

- Keep your legs uncrossed and planted firmly on the ground.

- Be still—relaxed, but not rock solid.

Also be careful that your body language is welcoming rather than intimidating. We've all seen people who stretch out by leaning back in their chairs or extending their arms over neighboring chairs. They're showing disrespect by taking up more space than they should and leaning back as though they're outside the group conversation. Dominant stances can also be a problem in one-on-one conversations. Let's say you're a manager and you come to the desk of one of your staff. You put your hands on the individual's desk and lean over that person. You've adopted an intimidating stance. There's no way the subordinate will

share an idea or speak openly to you because of the physical power dynamic you've created.

Nor do you want to project a submissive stance. Some people—because of habit, socialization, or insecurity—make themselves small by taking up less than their full chair, rounding their backs, lowering their heads, and crossing their legs. This behavior does not serve them well. It makes them appear inconsequential. Such body language can signal that you are not confident in what you are saying.

As a leader, it's imperative to show a strong, confident stance whether sitting or standing. So take up your rightful place and own your space.

Lead with Gestures

Next, make sure your gestures convey your leadership. The key here is "open" gestures. They not only add force to what you say, but they also show that you are listening and accessible. They indicate you are trustworthy and have nothing to hide. Your arms will do a lot of talking for you! To achieve this openness:

- Never cross your arms—you will look defensive or closed.
- Gesture with your full arms extended toward your audience.
- Avoid "flipper" gestures from elbows tucked into your body.
- Avoid busy wrist gestures and fleeting movements.
- Keep your hands open, don't hold them together, fold them, or flatten them on the table.

Openness is paramount. Imagine a boss asking her team for new ideas as she stands in front of them with her arms crossed. Her voice says, "What are your ideas?" but her body declares, "I am not open to what you think." Or let's say you're in the elevator and your boss walks

in, and you immediately close your arms and fold your hands. You'll appear defensive and afraid. Arms crossed connote "armor," protecting you from others around you.

Open gestures should be scaled to the ideas you're delivering and the size of your audience. The bigger the idea and the larger the audience, the fuller your gestures. In a meeting with 10 to 12 colleagues, big gestures (the size of a beach ball) will be more effective than small gestures that won't be felt by the room. In a one-on-one meeting, smaller gestures are typically more appropriate. But if you're making a key point, or demonstrating your passion for an idea, you can use expansive gestures.

Your open gestures should also be nuanced by your personality and immediate goals. If you want to come across as a confident professional—for example, in a job interview—your gestures will most aptly be warm, yet firm and authoritative, reflecting strong leadership qualities. If you want to come across as a daring thinker, your gestures will be more expansive. Entrepreneurs like Richard Branson, Elon Musk, and Jeff Bezos often have exciting, bold movements that show their dynamic personalities. If you want to build rapport with the people around you in an informal situation, you can be relaxed and more personal with your gestures, reaching out to them, nodding your head in agreement, and, in some rare cases, touching.

Avoid the following gestures that convey negative messages:

- Aggressive gestures (closed fists, a pointed finger, or a raised hand).
- Nervous gestures (wringing hands, jingling coins, or fidgeting).
- Minimizing gestures (using your hand to hide your face, cover your mouth, or hold your neck self-protectively).
- Grooming gestures (stroking or tossing your hair, touching or stroking your face).

Gestures are a powerful way of building a relationship with your audience. They speak for you and show others you want to connect with them. In each impromptu encounter, think about how they can best serve you.

Use the Power of Your Eyes

Eye contact is another powerful aspect of body language. Seventy percent of our body's sense receptors are in our eyes.[2] We take in with our eyes more than twice the information we receive from all our other senses put together. Our eyes also tell our audience a lot about us. If we make strong and warm eye contact, they're more likely to see us as approachable, likeable, trustworthy, and believable. And, according to a joint study by the University of Wolverhampton and the University of Stirling, eye contact increases the audience's retention of what we're saying.[3]

Getting it right can make all the difference in impromptu exchanges. Here's how you can use your eyes to strengthen your communication.

First, use them to study your audience, whether it's one person or many, to make sure you're getting your message across. If your listeners seem distracted, that might mean you're moving through your material too quickly or too slowly. So adjust your pace. It also could mean you haven't got the message right. Take that feedback and adjust on the fly. You might say, "Do you want me to run that by you again?" or you might simply restate your point in different words. That's what the best spontaneous exchanges are about.

Second, be sure you're looking at your audience when you drive home each point. It's not necessary to look at the other person 100 percent of the time. No listener wants us to stare at them constantly.

Indeed, when we're searching for our ideas in impromptu speaking, we often drop our eyes or look to the side to think. But at the end of every sentence or idea, come back to your audience and make eye contact.

And as you look at them, silently ask, "Did you get that?" While your audience won't hear you say those words, your gaze and your intention that they "get" what you just said will ground them in that idea, and make it more memorable to them. It's similar to a golf swing. A golfer has to continue the swing all the way around, well past the shoulder, or the ball won't go in the right direction. This same follow-through is necessary in speaking if you want the audience to receive each idea.

Third, use your eyes to "own the room." Many people look out into space when they're talking to a group—rather than looking at specific people. Our eyes often go to the ceiling, the walls, the table, and even the door when someone walks in. This "walkabout" with our eyes disconnects us from our audience. The secret is to make one-on-one eye contact with the people you're talking to. Even if you have fifteen people in the room, do your best to focus on one person at a time. As you deliver one idea, choose someone who is looking at you and make eye contact with them. Then deliver the next thought to another person. Keep going around the room and make one-on-one eye contact with each person—or at least as many as you can. This person-to-person connection will enable you to hold the room.

Fourth, show with your eyes that you're listening while *others* speak. Our gaze shows we are alert, engaged, and responsive. So whether you are in a one-on-one hallway conversation, or in a meeting with ten people, keep your eyes focused on the speaker, and make clear that you are interested in what that individual is saying. You'll be perceived as a good listener, and you'll become one as well.

Eye contact is a powerful—if not the most powerful—aspect of your body language. It helps you to build a strong relationship with everyone. Remember, "the eyes have it!" Use them well.

Put Your Best Face Forward

Finally, getting your facial expression right is a key aspect of impromptu leadership. Here are the things to keep in mind.

Begin with a warm, collegial, and empathetic expression if you want to persuade or inspire others. Nobody will follow you if you look like you don't care about them. This warmth cannot be "put on." It must be genuinely felt. It's reflected in a smile—not a big, happy smile that's plastered on your face. I mean a smile that is grounded in your feelings. I like to think of it as an "inner smile." It will give your audience a good feeling about you, and give you a warmth and overall presence.

Second, make sure your face reflects what you are saying. Who hasn't seen someone in a meeting—or a TV anchor—beaming her way through a set of remarks that on balance are negative or neutral? For example, imagine a manager telling her colleagues in a perky tone, with a wide smile on her face, "We won't be meeting our quarterly sales targets." Clearly the face is trying to hide the reality or the speaker is more concerned about being cheerful than about delivering a grounded message. Don't let this happen to you.

Third, keep your face unobstructed and available to your audience.

- Don't let your hair hang in your face.
- Don't touch your face or rub it.
- Don't hold your face in your hands.
- Don't turn your face away from your audience.
- Don't drop your face while you're speaking.
- Don't turn or drop your face when someone is talking.

Body language is truly a language of its own—and it's one that conveys your feelings and intentions alongside your words. Follow the advice in this chapter and make sure your stance, gestures, eyes, and facial expression all support and reinforce your leadership.

CONCLUSION

DON'T BE SCARED, BE PREPARED

There are two types of speakers: those that are nervous, and those that are liars.

—Mark Twain

When I tell people I've written a work on impromptu speaking, the most common response is, "I could use that book. I get really scared when I have to speak extemporaneously."

Why is "impromptu" so frightening?

In part, it's the fear of the unknown. There is a generalized fear when we hear the word "impromptu" that anyone could throw us anything at any time. That takes us out of our comfort zone. We lose control, and we humans like to have control. We're afraid that we will open our mouth and have nothing to say—either nothing at all, or nothing that makes any sense. And we are afraid of being judged—afraid of what others will think of us. A client told us she experiences mind freeze when she presents to executives. She's afraid of being criticized by her superiors, so she mentally retreats. Experiencing mind freeze—or its opposite, blathering on and on without coherence—can happen in any meeting, hallway conversation, or high-stakes situation like a job interview. The outcome can be deep disappointment. Who has not

followed up an impromptu event with "Why did I say that?" or "Why *didn't* I say that?"

Even the most seasoned executives can have tremors about speaking in off-the-cuff situations. A vice president our firm was working with confided that "the one challenge I would like to overcome is being able to stand up at a meeting of 250 vice presidents and the CEO of my company and say, 'I have an idea.' Or, 'This is my thinking on the subject.'" He said he'd like to overcome that initial stage fright. "Once I get up I'll be fine because I know my subject," he said. "But still that feeling of standing up and being exposed, being on stage is nerve-racking, so I tend not to take the initiative and stand up."

Developing these skills, as this book has shown, involves *preparing* for spontaneity. This will ensure that you are confident, focused, "on message," and inspiring whatever the circumstances. This ability is at the core of leadership.

Prepare, Prepare, Prepare

My call to action to you is this: build your impromptu skills by preparing in every way you can. This is a message that has been internalized and demonstrated by countless leaders. Let me leave you with the following "to-do" list so you can excel as an impromptu leader and inspire your team, your clients, your executives, and all who have the privilege of listening to you speak in the corridors and meeting rooms of your daily life.

First, develop the mind-set of a leader. Begin today to cultivate an outlook that will turn spontaneous encounters into leadership moments. Ask yourself, "Am I intent on leading, and how can I choose my best leadership moments?" "Am I a good listener?" "How can I be more authentic?" "Is my mind focused when I talk to people?" "Do I think respectfully of my boss, colleagues, and company?"

These questions form a valuable checklist, and suggest the qualities to cultivate if you want to show your audience that you are a caring and compelling leader.

Second, internalize the Leader's Script. If you master this template and its components, you'll have a firm foundation for structuring your thinking in any impromptu situation. It helps, of course, to know your subject and have some key messages in mind to draw upon. But it is fundamentally important to internalize the elements of the Leader's Script—grabber, message, structure, and call to action. Whether you have a week, an hour, or merely moments to create your impromptu remarks, this template will enable you to respond to any situation with clear thinking.

Third, script yourself for each occasion. Once you know you're going to be "on"—at a networking event, a job interview, a meeting with your boss, or a conversation in the elevator—use whatever time you have to craft your remarks. The sample impromptu scripts in this book will provide a guide to creating tailored remarks for virtually any occasion. And the more you use these models, the more readily they will come to mind when you only have a few seconds to think.

Fourth, develop your presence. Use the techniques discussed in the last section of this book to strengthen your leadership presence, so when the time comes for an important interview, networking event, or Q&A, you'll project strength and confidence. Rehearse whenever you can. Be alert to the words you use. Master improv techniques so you can be "in the moment." Know how to use your voice and body to express your leadership.

A Little Help from Our Unconscious Mind

You may be asking yourself, "When the time comes for me to pull all this together on the spot, will I be able to do it? In the blink of an eye? It might sound overwhelming.

The good news is that when speaking impromptu we do not have to consciously work through everything discussed in this book. As Malcolm Gladwell tells us in *Blink: The Power of Thinking Without Thinking*, we don't make all these split-second decisions consciously, we make them unconsciously. He writes: "The part of our brain that leaps to conclusions like this is called the adaptive unconscious. . . . a kind of giant computer that quickly and quietly processes a lot of the data we need in order to keep functioning as human beings."[1] Gladwell explains that this adaptive unconscious is responsible for the split-second decisions that are made by doctors in the ER room, by improvisational actors when deciding on their next line, and by professional basketball players when making unbelievable three-point shots in a flash. The same "thinking without thinking" split-second decision-making is available to us when we pause before speaking impromptu.

Improvisational acting and music provide strong parallels with impromptu speaking. "Improv isn't random and chaotic at all," Gladwell explains. Indeed, "improv is an art form governed by a series of rules, and [actors] want to make sure that when they're up onstage, everyone abides by those rules."[2] The same holds true for jazz music. As Stephen T. Asma, who once jammed with rhythm and blues great Bo Diddley, writes: "In music, improvising with others requires a language of musical tools and norms." "The ability to improvise," Asma explains, "is not just 'winging it.' It is built on foundations of study and practice that prepare the improviser for the moment of action."[3] Impromptu speaking requires the same discipline that the best improvisational actors and jazz musicians use. It, too, is built on a set of rules as well as practice. This emphasis on preparation forms the essence of this book. Preparing to be spontaneous may seem like a contradiction in terms—a counterintuitive thought—but it is the only way to be a superb impromptu speaker.

Few skills are more important today for leaders and aspiring leaders than the ability to speak well in impromptu situations. The day when executives could deliver the big speech and then retreat to their offices is long gone. Constant, spontaneous interactions with colleagues, senior executives, clients, and stakeholders have become the norm. Elevator conversations can be career-defining moments. Information is exchanged in "real time." And despite the flood of emails that wash over us, face-to-face exchanges have become ever more important.

The extraordinary importance of impromptu speaking is why I've written this book, and why mastering this skill is crucial for everyone, at every level in an organization.

This book provides a clear and consistent approach to becoming an excellent spontaneous speaker. Apply the principles set forth to every situation. Internalize them as your go-to strategies for impromptu speaking. Embrace the many small stages that present themselves every day in your business and personal life. Speaking well in impromptu situations has become one of the crucial skills that every leader today must master. The new world of leadership is full of conversation, collaboration, and charisma.

Make the most of these opportunities.

ENDNOTES

Opening Quotation

J. V. Muir, ed., *Alcidamas: The Works and Fragments* (London: Bristol Classical Press, 2001), 7.

Introduction

1. Johanna Schneller, "oscars' epic Best Picture fail a Hollywood metaphor," February 27, 2017, https://www.thestar.com/entertainment/television/2017/02/27/oscars-epic-best-picture-fail-a-hollywood-metaphor.html.

2. *La La Land* producer Jordan Horowitz on Oscars best picture mix-up, ABC News, February 27, 2917. http://abcnews.go.com/GMA/video/la-la-land-producer-jordan-horowitz-oscars-best-45776196.

3. Tim Webb, "BP's clumsy response to oil spill threatens to make a bad situation worse," *The Guardian*, June 1, 2010; https://www.theguardian.com/business/2010/jun/01/bp-response-oil-spill-tony-hayward.

4. Online Etymology Dictionary, http://www.etymonline.com/index.php?term=impromptu.

5. The Story of Caedmon's Hymn is told by Bede in his *Ecclesiastical History of the English People [Historia ecclesiastica gentis Anglorum]*, Book IV, Chapter xxiv, Cambridge, University Library Kk.5.16, fol.128b.

6. Abraham Lincoln, "Notes for a Law Lecture," as quoted in David Herbert Donald, *Lincoln* (New York: Touchstone, 1995), 98.

7. Donald T. Phillips, *Lincoln on Leadership: Executive Strategies for Tough Times* (New York: Warner Books, 1993), 145.

8. Lord Moran, *Churchill: Taken from the Diaries of Lord Moran* (Boston, 1966), 132. Passage quoted in Kathleen Hall Jamieson, *Eloquence in an Electronic Age* (New York: Oxford University Press, 1988), 4.

9. Pastor Terrell Harris, "The Preaching of Martin Luther King Jr.," The Opened Box, January 20, 2014, http://theopenedbox.com/articles/the-preaching-of-martin-luther-king-jr/.

10. Clayborne Carson, ed., *The Autobiography of Martin Luther King, Jr.* (New York: Warner Books, 1998), 223.

11. Richard Branson, "How to overcome public speaking nerves," Virgin.com, https://www.virgin.com/entrepreneur/richard-branson-how-overcome-public-speaking-nerves.

12. Carmine Gallo, "Branson, Buffett Agree: This Skill Is Your Ticket to Career Success," forbes.com, Feb. 18, 2016, http://www.carminegallo.com/branson-buffett-agree-this-skill-is-your-ticket-to-career-success/.

13. Elon Musk, in an interview at Silicon Valley's Churchill Club, quoted by Carmine Gallo in "Richard Branson: 'Communication Is the Most Important Skill Any Leader Can Possess," Forbes.com, July 7, 2015, http://www.forbes .com/sites/carminegallo/2015/07/07/richard-branson-communication-is-the-most-important-skill-any-leader-can-possess. . . .

14. Carmine Gallo, "Branson, Buffett Agree: This Skill Is Your Ticket to Career Success," Ibid.

15. The 2017 Berkshire Hathaway Annual Shareholders Meeting, Omaha, Nebraska, broadcast by Yahoo!Finance, May 6, 2017. https://finance.yahoo .com/BRKlivestream/.

16. https://www.youtube.com/watch?v=lGE1vyW5Y5Y

Chapter 1 – The Rise of Impromptu Speaking

1. Elon Musk, tweet, April 6, 2016, https://twitter.com/elonmusk/status/717749079707484160.

2. Vivian Giang, "What Kind of Leadership Is Needed in Flat Hierarchies?" *Fast Company*, May 19, 2015, https://www.fastcompany.com/3046371/what-kind-of-leadership-is-needed-in-flat-hierarchies.

3. Deborah Ancona and Henrik Bresman, *X-Teams: How to Build Teams That Lead, Innovate, and Succeed* (Boston: Harvard Business School Press, 2007), 9.

4. Ibid., 42.

5. Rick Levine, Christopher Locke, Doc Searls, and David Weinberger, *The Cluetrain Manifesto* (New York: Basic Books, 2009), xvii.

6. Greene quoted in Harry McCracken, "'At Our Scale, It's Important to Focus,'" *Fast Company*, December 2016/January 2017, 103.

7. Thomas Petzinger, Jr., Foreword, *The Cluetrain Manifesto*, xi.

8. Joseph McCormack, *Brief* (Hoboken, New Jersey: John Wiley & Sons, 2014), 16.

9. Rachel Emma Silverman, "Where's the Boss? Trapped in a Meeting," *Wall Street Journal*, February 14, 2012.

10. Gloria Mark, Victor M. Gonzalez, and Justin Harris, "No Task Left Behind? Examining the Nature of Fragmented Work," https://www.researchgate.net/publication/221516226_No_Task_Left_Behind_Examining_the_Nature_of_Fragmented_Work, 324.

11. Seth Stevenson, "The Boss with No Office," *Slate*, May 4, 2014, http://www.slate.com/articles/business/psychology_of_management/2014/05/open.plan.office.

12. Alex Bozikovic, "FACEBOOK, U.S.A.," *The Globe and Mail*, June 22, 2016, for "building as village" concept. See also Adam Lashinsky, Mark Zuckerberg, *Fortune*, December 1, 2016, 70 for description of "glass walls" that surround Zuckerberg's office.

13. Om Malik, "Jennifer Magnolfi," https://pi.co/jennifer-magnolfi-work-office-spaces.

Chapter 2 – The Power of Spontaneity

1. Conor Dougherty, "Innovator in Chief," *New York Times*, January 24, 2016, Sunday Business, 1, 4.

2. Joseph McCormack, *Brief* (Hoboken, New Jersey: John Wiley & Sons, 2014), 19.

3. Interview with Boris Groysberg and Michael Slind, "How Effective Leaders Talk (and Listen)," *HBR IdeaCast*, July 5, 2012, https://hbr.org/2012/07/how-effective-leaders-talk-and-listen.

4. Adam Lashinsky, "Zuckerberg," *Fortune*, December 1, 2016, 70–71.

5. Ibid., 70.

6. Harry McCracken, "At Our Scale, It's Important to Focus," *Fast Company*, December 2016/January 2017, 72.

7. Jeff Immelt, "Why GE Is Giving up Employee Ratings, Abandoning Annual Reviews and Rethinking the Role of HQ," LinkedIn, August 4, 2016.

8. Rick Levine, Christopher Locke, Doc Searls, and David Weinberger, *The Cluetrain Manifesto* (New York: Basic Books, 2009), 1.

9. Patrick Lencioni, *The Advantage* (San Francisco: Jossey-Bass, 2012), 147.

10. Theodore Sorensen, *Kennedy* (New York: Bantam Books, 1966), 200.

11. John Birmingham, "Unscripted: 21 Ad-Libs that Became Classic Movie Lines," April 19, 2017, www.purpleclover.com/entertainment/4792-ultimate-ad-libs/.

12. William von Hippel, Richard Ronay, Ernest Baker, Kathleen Kjelsaas, and Sean C. Murphy, "Quick Thinkers Are Smooth Talkers," *Psychological Science*, November 30, 2015, https://www.psychologicalscience.org/news/releases/quick-thinkers-are-charismatic.html. Abstract of research, "Quick Thinkers Are Smooth Talkers: Mental Speed Facilitates Charisma," http://sagepub.com/doi/full/10.1177/0956797615616255.

13. Julie Beck, "Quick Thinkers Seem Charismatic, Even If They're Not That Smart," *The Atlantic*, December 4, 2015, https://theatlantic.com/health/archive/2015/12/quick-thinkers-seem-charismatic-even-if-they're-not-that-smart/418629/. Author draws upon the study by William von Hippel et al. (see note 12).

14. Stephen T. Asma, "Was Bo Diddley a Buddha?" *New York Times*, April 10, 2017, https://www.nytimes.com/2017/04/10/opinion/was-bo-diddley-a-budda.

Chapter 3 – Be Intent on Leading

1. Daniel Ford, "Gallup: 70 Percent of U.S. Workers Are Disengaged," *Associations Now*, June 13, 2013, http://associationsnow.com/2013/06/gallup-workplace-study-finds-majority-of-u-s-workers-are-disengaged/.

2. Walter Isaacson, *Steve Jobs* (New York: Simon & Schuster, 2011), 38, 561, 564.

3. James Covert and Claire Atkinson, "'No layoffs … this week': Marissa Mayer's creepy comment kills morale," *New York Post*, January 18, 2016. (Italics in quoted passage mine.)

4. Patrick Lencioni, *The Advantage* (San Francisco: Jossey-Bass, 2012), 149.

5. Trudeau's 'because it's 2015' retort draws international attention," The Canadian Press, November 5, 2015. https://www.theglobeandmail.com/news/po https://www.theglobeandmail.com/news/politics/trudeaus-because-its-2015-retort-draws-international-cheers/article27119856/.tlitics/trudeaus-because-its-2015-retort-draws-international-cheers/article27119856/.

6. Conor Friedersdorf, "The Gettysburg Address at 150—and Lincoln's Impromptu Words the Night Before," *The Atlantic*, November 19, 2013, https://www.theatlantic.com/politics/archive/2013/11/the-gettysburg-address-at-150-and-lincoln's-impromptu-words-the-night-before-281606/.

7. Ahiza Garcia, "Carrier workers' rage over move to Mexico caught on video," CNN Money, February 19, 2016, http://money.cnn.com/2016/02/12/news/companies/carrier-moving-jobs-mexico-youtube/index.html.

8. Rosabeth Moss Kanter, *Evolve!* (Boston: Harvard Business School Press, 2001), p. 7.

Chapter 4 – Be a Listener

1. Epictetus was a Greek Stoic philosopher who lived from 50 to 135 AD. Born a slave, he studied philosophy and eventually taught philosophy in Rome for twenty-five years.

2. Om Malik, "Jennifer Magnolfi," https://pi.co/jennifer-magnolfi-work-office-spaces/, 8.

3. Seth Stevenson, "The Boss with No Office," *Slate*, May 4, 2014, http://www.slate.com/articles/business/psychology_of_management/2014/05/open_plan_offices_the_new_trend_in_workplace_design.html.

4. Joseph McCormack, *Brief* (Hoboken, New Jersey: John Wiley & Sons, 2014), 19.

5. McKinsey Global Institute, "The Social Economy: Unlocking Value and Productivity through Social Technologies," cited in Jena McGregor, "How much time you really spend emailing at work," *Washington Post*, July 31, 2012, https://www.washingtonpost.com/blogs/post-leadership/post/how-much-time-you-really-spend-emailing-at-work/2012/07/31/gJQAI50sMX_blog.html?utm_term=.12be059f46c2.

6. Aaron Smith, "Americans and Text Messaging," September 19, 2011, Pew Research Center, http://pewinternet.org/2011/09/19/americans-and-textmessaging/.

7. Maria Gonzalez, *Mindful Leadership* (Mississauga, Ontario: Jossey-Bass, 2012), 31.

8. Ibid., 127.

9. Richard Branson, interview with Chase Jarvis "Creative Live," May 10, 2016, https://www.youtube.com/watch?v=ubHMuYjUCfU.

10. Cindi May, "A Learning Secret: Don't Take Notes with a Laptop," *Scientific American*, June 3, 2014, http://www.scientificamerican.com/article/a-learning-secret-don't-t.

11. Natalie Baker, "Your employees wish you were emotionally intelligent," *The Economist*, April 5, 2016, httsp://execed.economist.com/blog/industry-trends/your-employees-wish-you-were-emotionally-intelligent.

12. Dr. Seuss, *Seuss-isms: Wise and Witty Prescriptions for Living from the Good Doctor* (New York: Random House, 1997).

Chapter 5 – Be Authentic

1. James M. Kouzes and Barry Z. Posner, *Credibility: How Leaders Gain and Lose It, Why People Demand It* (San Francisco: Jossey-Bass, 2011), xi.

2. Adam Grant, "Unless You're Oprah, 'Be Yourself' Is Terrible Advice," *New York Times*, Sunday Review, June 4, 2016.

3. Online Etymology Dictionary, http://www.etymonline.com/index.php?term=authentic.

4. Rob Goffee and Gareth Jones, *Why Should Anyone Be Led By You?* (Boston: Harvard Business Review Press, 2015), x.

5. Elon Musk, interview at D11 Conference, May 29, 2013, https://www.youtube.com/watch?v=UiPO4BUfov8&feature=youtu.be&t=18mRosab3s.

6. Simon Sinek, *Start with Why* (New York: Penguin Group, 2009), 133.

7. Rosabeth Moss Kanter, *Evolve!* (Boston: Harvard University Press, 2001), 267.

8. Walter Isaacson, *Steve Jobs* (New York: Simon & Schuster, 2011), 565.

9. Patrick Lencioni, *The Advantage* (San Francisco: Jossey-Bass, 2012), 27.

10. Marla Tabaka, "Four Success Lessons From Amazon's Jeff Bezos," Inc.com, August 18, 2015, http://www.inc.com/marla-tabaka/4-success-lessons-from-jeff-bezos. . . .

11. Eugene Kim, "How the CEO of this $2.5 billion tech company hires without asking many questions," *Business Insider*, April 23, 2016, http://www.businessinsider.com/shopify-ceo-interview-question-2016–4.

12. Jack Dorsey, interview at Oxford Union Society, April 8, 2015, https://www.youtube.com/watch?v=uB3xns-E48c.

13. Warren Bennis, *On Becoming a Leader* (New York: Basic Books, 2009), 45–46.

Chapter 6 – Be Focused

1. Joseph McCormack, *Brief* (Hoboken, New Jersey: John Wiley & Sons, 2014), 16.

2. Rick Stengel, managing editor, *Time*, interview with Mark Zuckerberg; time .com/video, http://content.time.com/time/video/player/0,32068,7110478700 01_2037225,00.html.

3. "Attention Span Statistics," National Center for Biotechnology Information, July 2, 2016, http://www.statisticbrain.com/attention-span-statistics/.

4. Christopher Hooton, *Independent*, "Our Attention Span Is Now Less Than That of a Goldfish, Microsoft Study Finds," May 13, 2015. http:// www.independent.co.uk/news/science/our-attention-span-is-now-less-than-a-goldfish-microsoft-study-finds-10247553html.

5. Mark Goulston, "How to Know If You Talk Too Much," *Harvard Business Review*, June 3, 2015. https://hbr.org/2015/06/how-to-know-if-you-talk-too-much.

6. This example has been slightly altered so as not to identify the actual CEO.

7. Theodore Sorensen, *Kennedy* (New York: Bantam Books, 1966), 365.

8. Churchill quoted in *Manner of Speaking*, "Quotes for Public Speakers" (No. 112), https://mannerofspeaking.org/2012/01/06/quotes-for-public-speakers-no-112/.

Chapter 7 – Be Respectful

1. "Daniel Craig quits as James Bond for US series," *Bang Showbiz*, February 16, 2016, http://www.msn.com/en-ca/entertainment/celebrity/daniel-craig-quits-as-james-bond-for-us-series/ar-BBpw5wV.

2. James Kouzes and Barry Posner, *Credibility* (San Francisco: John Wiley & Sons, 2011), 92.

3. Ben Widdicombe, "What Happens When Millennials Run the Workplace?" *New York Times*, March 19, 2016, http://nyti.ms/1RaeMw4.

Chapter 8 – Lay the Groundwork

1. Colin Perkel, the *Canadian Press*, "PM Smarty-Pants: Trudeau delivers impromptu computing lesson," April 15, 2016, Canada.com, http://bit.ly/2bssEZU.

2. Charles Bramesco, "Man of Your Dreams Justin Trudeau Casually Drops Quantum Computing Lecture in Press Conference," *Vanity Fair*, April 16, 2016, http://www.vanityfair.com/news/2016/04/justin-trudeau-quantum-computing.

3. For nineteenth-century use of paper cuffs to write on, see *Early Sports and Pop Culture Blog*, "Paper Linen and Crib Notes—A Well-Planned History of 'Off the Cuff,'" February 20, 2015. For Oxford English Dictionary (OED) confirmation of first use and origin of off-the-cuff speaking see: http://languagelog.ldc.upenn.edu/nll/?p=4130.

4. "Demosthenes: Introduction to Demosthenes," http://erenow.com/ancient/the-age-of-alexander/7.html.

5. "Three Weeks to Prepare a Good Impromptu Speech," http://quoteinvestigator.com/2010/06/09/twain-speech.

6. James C. Humes, *Speak Like Churchill, Stand Like Lincoln* (New York: Three Rivers Press, 2002), 26.

7. James C. Humes, *Sir Winston Method* (New York: William, 1991), 169–170.

8. Carmine Gallo, *The Presentation Secrets of Steve Jobs* (New York: McGraw Hill, 2010), 199.

9. Jillian Rayfield, "Eastwood explains why he spoke to the chair," http://www.salon.com/2012/09/07/eastwood. According to an article published in *The Washington Post*, written by Travis M. Andrews, August 4, 2016 (http://wpo.st/uiVq1—see file), Eastwood retracted his 2012 explanation and said he regretted "that silly thing at the Republican convention, talking to the chair."

10. Kathleen Hall Jamieson, *Eloquence in an Electronic Age* (New York: Oxford University Press, 1988), 232.

11. Adam Lashinsky, "Facebook CEO Mark Zuckerberg," *Fortune*, December 1, 2016, 71.

12. Zuckerberg quotations are from a variety of sources. The first is from an interview with Sam Altman, "How to Build the Future," August 16, 2016, https://www.scribd.com/document/321383212/How-to-Build-the-Future-Mark-Zuckerberg#download&from_embed. The second, third, and fourth are from Zuckerberg's F8 2016 keynote presentation, http://www.singjupost.com/facebook-ceo-mark-zuckerberg-at-f8–2016. The last is from a 2010 interview with Rick Stengel, *Time*, http://content.time.com/time/video/player/0,32068,711047870001_2037225,00.html.

13. Adam Lashinsky, "Facebook CEO Mark Zuckerberg," *Fortune*, December 1, 2016, 70–71.

Chapter 9 – Read Your Audience

1. Candace West, "Against Our Will: Male Interruptions of Females in Cross-Sex Conversations," *Annals of the New York Academy of Sciences* 327 (June 1979), 81–96. Men interrupted women 75 percent of the time in cross-sex conversations.

Chapter 10 – The Scripting Template

1. J. V. Muir, ed., *Alcidamas: The Works & Fragments* (London: Bristol Classical Press, 2001), 7.

2. H. L. Hudson-Williams, *Greece & Rome,* Vol. 18, No. 52 (Cambridge University Press, Jan. 1949), 30, http://www.jstor.org/stable/641798.

3. Michael de Brauw, "The Parts of the Speech," in *A Companion to Greek Rhetoric*, ed., Ian Worthington (Malden, Massachusetts: Blackwell Publishing, 2007), 187–199.

4. "Richard Branson on the Art of Public Speaking," *Entrepreneur*, February 16, 2013, http://www.entrepreneurmag.co.za/advice/personal-improvement/self-development/richard-branson-on-the-art-of-public-speaking/.

Chapter 11 – Commit to a Message

1. Cartoon by Mike Baldwin, for "Cornered," *The Globe and Mail*, May 29, 2017.

2. Rick Tetzeli, "The Real Legacy of Steve Jobs, *Fast Company*, April 2015, 73.

3. Harry McCracken, "At Our Scale, It's Important to Focus," *Fast Company*, December 2016 /January 2017, 72.

4. Marla Tabaka, "Four Success Lessons from Amazon's Jeff Bezos," Inc.com, August 18, 2015. http://www.inc.com/marla-tabaka/4-success-lessons-from-jeff-bezos. The article cites an interview Bezos had with *Time*.

Chapter 12 – Make a Compelling Case

1. Tom Quirk, referring to William Dean Howells's "divine ragbag" comment about Twain's approach to composing, in Introduction, *Mark Twain: Tales, Speeches, Essays and Sketches*, ed., Tom Quirk (New York: Penguin Books, 1994), xiii.

2. Duff McDonald, *Last Man Standing: The Ascent of Jamie Dimon and JPMorgan Chase* (New York: Simon & Schuster, 2009), 312.

Chapter 14 – Meetings

1. "Meetings in America," A Verizon Conferencing Whitepaper, https://emeetings .verizonbusiness.com/global/en/meetingsinamerica/uswhitepaper.php#COST.

2. See several sources: Ray Williams, "Why Meetings Kill Productivity," *Psychology Today*, https://www.psychologytoday.com/blog/wired-success/201204/why-meetings-kill-productivity; Bourree Lam, "The Wasted Workday," *The Atlantic*, December 4, 2014, https://www.theatlantic.com/business/archive/2014/12/the-wasted-workday/383380/; "Meetings in America," A Verizon Conferencing Whitepaper, https://e-meetings.verizonbusiness.com/global/en/meetingsinamerica/uswhitepaper.php#COST.

3. Oriana Bandiera, Luigi Guiso, Andrea Prat, and Raffaella Sadun, "What Do CEOs Do?" Cambridge: Harvard Business School Working Paper 11–081 (2011), www.hbs.edu/faculty/Publication%20Files/11–081.pdf. Cited in Joseph McCormack, *Brief* (Hoboken, New Jersey: John Wiley & Sons, 2014), 17.

Chapter 15 – Job Interviews, Networking, and Elevator Conversations

1. http://elevatorworldtour.com/about.html#.

Chapter 16 – "Just the Big Picture"

1. H. L. Hudson-Williams, "Impromptu Speaking," *Greece & Rome*, Vol. 18, No. 52 (Cambridge University Press, January, 1949), 28, http://www.jstor.org/stable/641798.

Chapter 17 – Toasts and Tributes

1. Larry Tye, *Bobby Kennedy: The Making of a Liberal Icon* (New York: Random House, 2016), 410.

2. William Safire, ed., *Lend Me Your Ears: Great Speeches in History* (New York: Norton, 1997), 215–216.

Chapter 18 – The Impromptu Speech

1. Jonathan Eig, *Luckiest Man: The Life and Death of Lou Gehrig* (New York: Simon and Schuster, 2005), 316.

2. The Official Website of Lou Gehrig, http:www.lougehrig.com/about/farwell .html.

3. Eleanor Gehrig and Joseph Durso, *My Luke and I* (New York: Signet, 1976), 173.

Chapter 19 – Q&A

1. H. L. Hudson-Williams, "Impromptu Speaking," *Greek & Rome,* Vol. 18, No. 52 (Cambridge University Press, January, 1949), 28, http://www.jstor.org/ stable/641798.

2. Trey Williams, "Mark Zuckerberg Resolves to Read a Book Every Other Week in 2015," January 5, 2015, Marketwatchhttp://www.marketwatch.com/story/ mark-zuckerberg-resolves-to-read-a-book-every-other-week-in-2015–2015– 01–05.

3. Adam Lashinsky, "Mark Zuckerberg," *Fortune*, December 1, 2016, 70.

4. Matt Levine interview with Brad Katsuyama, "Brad Katsuyama Q&A: 'I Don't Think We Would Have Survived If It Was Just Hype,'" Bloomberg Markets, October 12, 2016, https://www.bloomberg.com/features/2016-brad-katsuyama-interview/.

5. Roy P. Basler, ed., *Collected Works of Abraham Lincoln* (New Brunswick, New Jersey: Rutgers University Press, 1953), Vol. 3, p. 16.

6. Jo Best, "IBM Watson: The Inside Story of How the Jeopardy-Winning Super-computer Was Born, and What It Wants to Do Next," Techrepublic, n.d., http://www.techrepublic.com/article/ibm-watson-the-inside-story-of....

Chapter 20 – Rehearse Your Remarks

1. http://abcnews.go.com/blogs/politics/2011/11/rick-perrys-debate-lapse-oops-cant-remember-department-of-energy/.

2. Scott Bromley, "How Scripted Are the Interviews on Late Night Talk Shows?" The Chernin Group, https://www.quora.com/How-scripted-are-the-intews-on-late-night-talk-shows.

3. Denzel Washington accepts Cecil B. DeMille Award (2016); https://www
    .youtube.com/watch?v=yTqzj3dYUOo.

4. Carmine Gallo, "Richard Branson: Communication Is the Most Important
    Skill Any Leader Can Possess," *Forbes*, July 7, 2015, https://www.forbes.com/
    sites/carminegallo/2015/07/07/richard-branson-communication-is-the-most-
    important-skill-any-leader-can-possess/#23f59bc82e8a.

Chapter 21 – Choose Your Words

1. Robert I. Fitzhenry, ed., *The Fitzhenry & Whiteside Book of Quotations*
    (Markham, Ontario: Fitzhenry & Whiteside, 1993), 482.

2. Abraham Lincoln, quoted in F. B. Carpenter, *Six Months at the White House
    with Abraham Lincoln* (1866). Reprinted (Bedford, MA: Applewood Books,
    2008), 312.

3. Bart Egnal, *Leading Through Language* (Hoboken, New Jersey: John Wiley &
    Sons, 2016).

4. Winston Churchill, speech on receiving the *London Times* Literary Award,
    November 2, 1949, quoted in Richard Langworth, ed., *Churchill by Himself*
    (New York: Public Affairs, 2011), 61.

5. Howard Schultz, "Smell the Coffee: Starbucks CEO Talks Business,"
    London Business Forum, May 10, 2011, https://www.youtube.com/watch?
    v=83yInyY1KLs.

6. Jessica Shambora, "Amex CEO Ken Chenault: Define Reality and Give Hope,"
    May 12, 2009, http://fortune.com/2009/05/12/amex-ceo-ken-chenault-
    define-reality-and-give-hope/?iid=sr-link5.

Chapter 22 – Use Improv Techniques

1. Vivian Giang, "Why Top Companies and MBA Programs Are Teaching
    Improv," *Fast Company*, January 13, 2016, https://www.fastcompany.com/
    3055380/why-top-companies-and-mba-programs-are-teaching-improv.

2. Lisa Evans, "3 Ways Improv Can Improve Your Career," *Fast Company*,
    January 31, 2014, https://www.fastcompany.com/3025570/3-ways-improv-
    can-improve….

3. Mark Tutton, "Why Using Improvisation to Teach Business Skills Is No Joke,"
    CNN.com, February 18, 2010, http://www.cnn.com/2010/BUSINESS/02/
    18/improvisation.business….

4. Edward Zareh, "Follow the Fear: The Influence of Del Close," video, https://www.youtube.com/watch?v=3DQVLqxg4bw.

5. Jeff Bezos, Interview with Henry Blodget, *Business Insider's* Ignition 2014, https://www.youtube.com/watch?v=Xx92bUw7WX8.

Chapter 23 – Find Your Voice

1. Diane Ackerman, *A Natural History of the Senses* (New York: Vintage Books, 1991), 6.

2. Blake Green, "That Classic Voice, That Timeless Look," *Toronto Star*, December 19, 1999, D10.

3. Chris Anderson, *TED Talks: The Official TED Guide to Public Speaking* (Toronto: HarperCollins Publishers Ltd, 2016), 19.

4. Juliana Schroeder and Nicholas Epley, "The Science of Sounding Smart," *Harvard Business Review*, October 7, 2015. https:/hbr.org/2015/10/the-science-of-sounding-smart.

Chapter 24 – Master Body Language

1. Amy Cuddy, "Your Body Language Shapes Who You Are," TED Talk, filmed June 2010.

2. Diane Ackerman, *A Natural History of the Senses* (New York: Vintage Books, 1991), 230.

3. A. J. Harbinger, "Seven Things Everyone Should Know about the Power of Eye Contact," *Business Insider*, May 14, 2015. For Abstract of Study, "Effect of Gazing at the Camera during a Video Link on Recall," see https://www.ncbi.nlm.nih.gov/pubmed/16081035.

Conclusion: Don't Be Scared, Be Prepared

1. Malcolm Gladwell, *Blink: The Power of Thinking Without Thinking* (New York: Little, Brown and Company), 11.

2. Ibid., 113.

3. Stephen T. Asma, "Was Bo Diddley a Buddha?" *New York Times*, April 10, 2017. https://nyti.ms/2nZii5i.

ACKNOWLEDGMENTS

When I began writing this book, I had no idea how enlightening—and challenging—the project would be. As I spoke with my sources and reflected on my work with clients over the years, I became aware that impromptu speaking is more pervasive, more exacting, and more critical a skill than I had realized.

I am grateful to the many individuals who helped me see the need for this book and the role it can play in the lives of leaders.

My thanks go first to the hundreds of clients I've coached over the past thirty years. I kept notebooks of those sessions, and those journals provide the rich texture of this book. But more than that, my memory of working with these generous, talented leaders inspired me to write about this topic that was the subject of so many coaching sessions.

I also greatly appreciate the individuals who sat down with me when I began this project and shared their thinking in a series of interviews. These were stimulating, valuable conversations. For their wisdom, candor, and eloquence, I thank Adeola Adebayo, John Carrington, Dr. Allan Conway, Toni Ferrari, Stuart Forman, Ian Gordon, David Hahn, Mary Hundt, Sussannah Kelly, Phil Mesman, Grace Palombo, Nick Palombo, Jay Rosenzweig, Paul Vallée, Mary Vitug, Murray Wigmore, and Miyo Yamashita. As well I thank Marc-André Blanchard, Canada's Ambassador to the United Nations, and Jonathan Bloomberg, chief executive officer of BloombergSen, for their valuable contribution to the book.

Members of The Humphrey Group, with their rich and varied experience and backgrounds, encouraged me to pursue this project and provided insights that have made it a better book! I'm grateful to Bart Egnal, Rob Borg-Olivier, James Ramsay, Margo Gouley, and Emily Hemlow. Another member of The Humphrey "troupe," Dan Dumsha, generously cocreated with Angela Galanopoulos the chapter on improv techniques. Both Dan and Angela are improv actors who work for the Vancouver TheatreSports League, where they facilitate "Improv for Business" workshops, and teach in the Improv Comedy Institute.

Several individuals painstakingly pored over the entire manuscript and gave me invaluable feedback. Fang Yu provided editorial advice and occasionally said, "This won't work for millennials." Cynthia Ward, a vice president in The Humphrey Group, read through the entire manuscript and made sure it reflected The Humphrey Group's Intellectual Property and reputation. Steve Mitchell, who recently retired to Bowen Island off the coast of Vancouver, BC, broke away from his garden and idyllic life to give me some of the best writing advice I've ever had.

Fast Company has been a wonderful partner to me, and some of the material in this book is taken from articles I have written for that publication over the past several years. Rich Bellis, my *Fast Company* editor, has encouraged me to explore topics I wouldn't otherwise have thought of writing about. I'm grateful to him for his creative talent and strong editorial support. He also provided material for the chapter on meetings.

The Wiley/Jossey-Bass team have been a pleasure to work with and most accommodating. Editor Jeanenne Ray accepted my proposal immediately, and gave me two extensions when I needed them. The publisher's editorial, design, production, and marketing teams have been great to work with. I heartily recommend Wiley as a publishing house that produces quality products.

Finally, I'm pleased to acknowledge my great debt to my family. My older son, Bart Egnal, now heads The Humphrey Group as CEO, and has been building the company as I've turned my focus to writing about what we teach. He has inspired me with his thinking and his leadership of the company. My younger son, Ben Egnal, is an art director in the world of advertising. He and his partner, Fang Yu, contributed the hand-drawn title of this book and continue to inspire me with their entrepreneurship and design talent. Marc Egnal, my husband, has been a loving companion on this journey. He read every chapter, in some cases many times, offering valuable edits and suggestions. I'm delighted to dedicate this book to him. Not to be forgotten is Higgins, our family's beloved pug and my muse during the first half of this book. Sadly he is no longer with us but I know this book would have made him proud!

A book is a journey for the author—but it is also a gathering of people who share their knowledge, insights, and collaborative spark. I am deeply grateful to all those mentioned here who have taken this journey with me. They've strengthened this work and enriched the process for me. And now I invite readers to continue that journey.

INDEX